TEN SACKS OF RICE

TEN SACKS OF RICE

Copyright © 2002 Penelope Dale

First Published 2002 by Karis Publishing, Inc.
1019 Meredith Drive, Austin, Texas, USA

ISBN: 0-9718040-0-1

Unless otherwise indicated, biblical quotations are from
the New International Version, © 1973, 1978, 1984, by the
International Bible Society.

Cover design by Michelle Reed

Ten Sacks of Rice

Our Way to China

by

Penelope Dale

Penelope Dale
丁桂貞

DEDICATION

To my husband, Donald, whom the Lord took home to glory before this book was completed.

To my sons, Andrew, Robin and Tony, and their wives and children who are all very precious to me.

To my many friends around the world whose lives have touched and blessed mine over the years.

May God bless you all.

ACKNOWLEDGEMENTS

I want to thank Bruce Smith and Wu Ping for their many visits to help me on my computer. Without their willingness to come to my aid, I would have been lost before I even began. Then there was Marilyn Hill, one of our "Triple C" kids from the sixties. Marilyn turned out to be living in Austin and offered to come and help me by researching our old prayer letters, Triple C Newsletters, and books. Thank you, Marilyn.

I am also very grateful to my son Tony and his family, who live here in Austin. At different times, each one has helped me in different ways. They've mostly helped with computer problems, but now Tony and his oldest son, Jonathan, are taking the publishing responsibility off my shoulders. For this I am eternally grateful.

Lastly, I want to mention Susan Titus Osborn's Christian Communicator Manuscript Critique Service whose six-session email course, "Write for Publication," was a tremendous help to me. I would highly recommend it to any potential writers. Barbara Robidoux, one of their senior editors, critiqued my manuscript and gave me many helpful suggestions. Thank you, Barbara.

FOREWORD

by Brother Andrew, Open Doors

I can't be sure how old the boy was, but he had read the Bible. Now that he had read it, what next? Well, who better to ask than the author? So, the boy wrote a letter to God—after all, God had written him a "letter" first! It sounded like a good idea, but the boy soon realized he had a dilemma—what is God's address?! Rather than give up, the boy decided to send his letter to a mainstream magazine—perhaps they know where God lives and can forward it to Him. The magazine published this boy's letter: "Dear God, I have read your book, have you written anything else?"

Sadly enough, the majority of people today are in this boy's shoes! There are many who don't know about God's extensive library—the many letters that He has written. "Clearly, you are a letter from Christ . . . written not with pen and ink, but with the Spirit of the living God . . . carved not on stone, but on human hearts" (2 Cor. 3:3).

Some time ago, before I had written my first book, *God's Smuggler*, I stepped into the home of the Dale family. They were living in Taiwan, and this was my first trip to "Red China." They had asked me to pray with one of their sons. Before I began praying, there was something I needed to know. I asked the boy, "Do you see Jesus in your parents?" Without any hesitation he answered, "Yes."

That is why this book is so powerful. It tells the story of people in whom God has written his sequel–lives that we can "see Jesus" in. This book is so tremendously valuable. It should be read by everyone. All of us can become "a letter from Christ."

Think of the difference it would make in the world today if everyone followed the example of Donald and Penny Dale, living a life that is transparent and faithful–a living letter.

PREFACE

This book illustrates the wonders of God's guidance and providence down to the minutest details of everyday life. It is such a joy to walk with the Lord in intimate fellowship with Him day-by-day at a very practical level.

The title, Ten Sacks of Rice: Our Way to China, introduces the "tentmaker" concept. It shows through the lives of Donald and myself that God can make the seemingly impossible–possible. You'll find out why the mayor's offer of ten sacks of rice per month was more valuable than any amount of money he could have offered. You'll also taste the excitement of stepping into the unknown with the Lord and seeing Him open up doors.

Tentmakers, like Paul in the early church (Acts 18:1), are those who cross cultural barriers while continuing in their secular work in order to share the gospel with those who otherwise would never be reached. Closed countries become creative access countries when ordinary men and women are creative in their approach.

Deuteronomy 6:7-9 tells us how to teach our children and grandchildren God's commands: "Talk about them when you sit at home and when you walk along the road, when you lie down and when you get up. Tie them as symbols on your hands and bind them on your foreheads. Write them on the doorframes of your houses and on your gates." The following story tells how we sought to obey that admonition and live by the biblical principles that we found in the Word of God.

TABLE OF CONTENTS

Foreword

Preface

"To walk with God"

CHAPTER 1

BIRTH THROUGH BARTS
1924-1945

**"Train up a child in the way he should go, and when he is
old he will not turn from it."**
Proverbs 22:6

Family and friends often heard me say when they tried to play
with my dolls, "They are <u>not</u> dolls, they are Chinese people, I'm
going to be a nurse and go to China when I grow up." Where
did such thoughts come from? I was only three or four years old
at the time, and no one knew why I felt the way I did. Today I
know that God put those thoughts in my mind.

I was born in Christchurch, New Zealand on March 6th,
1924. Apart from having the hospital "Baby Book" that gives
details of my weight and how much milk I consumed, I know
nothing of my infancy. My parents were very poor. Father's
mental health had been unstable since the first World War, and
he had difficulty finding work. Things were hard for my parents
who had moved from England to New Zealand several years earlier to find "a better life" after the horrors of World War I.

Before I was two years old, mother and I were on the boat
back to England, sailing via the Panama Canal. It was a long
trip. Later, Dad was able to work his way back to UK on another

vessel. However, his mental health was such that he was soon back in the hospital, and my mother was compelled to find work. She became Matron of a boys' boarding school, a position she kept for some years.

Because of these family circumstances, I was sent to live with an old school friend of Mum's, Margaret Armitage (Marta), who had offered to become my guardian. Marta lived with her parents at Farnley Hall, near Leeds in Yorkshire. Her parents were well off, with a lovely home surrounded by beautiful grounds. This became my home for more than six years. Marta also looked after her niece, Margaret Schofield, whose parents were medical missionaries in Uganda. Eventually, it became apparent that two small children running around Farnley Hall was becoming too much stress for old Mrs. Armitage. So, Marta's parents built her a cottage at the far end of the long conservatory adjoining Farnley Hall. When that was completed, Marta, Margaret and I all moved into the cottage. Shortly after that, Miss Shafto, whom we children called "Nanna," joined the three of us at the Cottage.

I remember those years fondly. Every evening after I'd been given my "tea" (the last meal of the day for a young child in UK in those days, not a cup of tea!), I was dressed up in my pretty, dark-red velvet dress. Then, hand-in-hand with either Marta or Nanna, I was taken through the conservatory to Grandfather Armitage's special room. There I would sit on his knees while he read me Bible stories. I loved these times with Grandpa. When

I got a little older and was used to this routine, I was told to go through the conservatory on my own. I remember being afraid and running for all my worth, banging the doors behind me. There were at least five sections to this long conservatory. Each section felt different. From the conservatory, through the billiard room and the library, down a long passageway, turn right into the huge front hall, and right again into the safety of Grandpa's room, to crawl up on his knees. To my relief, Grandpa always sat there expectantly, Bible in hand, ready to read to me.

I also remember walking in the springtime to the bluebell woods and looking in wonder at the massive blue carpet that had suddenly appeared under the trees. Nanna and I loved that walk, and we often talked about the Creator who made these incredible beauties for us to enjoy. I remember enjoying my role as big sister and being allowed to push little Margaret in her pram so that she could join us in our walks, even though she was too young to really appreciate the beauty of the world around her.

Farnley Hall, the Cottage, the beautiful grounds, and the walks with Nanna are not all my memories. A few weeks before Christmas we were always allowed to go to the "Big Kitchen" to stir the Christmas Pudding with Gal. This was an annual event that must never be missed; though I really did not like to eat the Christmas Pudding when weeks later it was put on the table.

A long garage sat behind the main building. It probably would have taken ten cars, and in those days it always housed at least one horse-drawn buggy. Alfred was chief chauffeur, and redheaded Raymond was the number two man in the garage department. The cars were always spotlessly clean. They must have been washed, waxed, and polished at least once every day. Alfred was designated to take me to school in Harrogate. I don't remember why I didn't go to school in Leeds, which was much closer. We occupied the time each day by trying a different route. I especially enjoyed going past the racing track where the old cars were often racing at tremendous speeds, or so it seemed to my five-year-old mind. Sometimes on the way home, I would persuade Alfred to stop beside the road and watch the cars for a few minutes.

One thing indelibly impressed on my young mind was the ritual of morning prayers. They were held in the sitting room and included everyone from the oldest to the youngest. The maids, about ten of them, trooped in in their pink dresses, white aprons, white caps, black shoes and stockings. Alfred and Raymond were there along with Gal and the cooks and, of course, all the Armitage family who were in residence at the time. Marta always sat at the piano at the far end of the room, while I sat beside Grandpa awed by the solemnity of it all. I think I must partially attribute my lifelong habit of daily prayer and Bible reading to these wonderful times with the whole Armitage household. For the Bible clearly tells us, "Train up a child in the way he should go, and when he is old he will not depart from it" (Proverbs 22:6). What a privilege was my childhood!

Driving to school with Alfred continued for several more years. I do not remember anything about those schools, but I do remember the great longing I had to own my own bicycle. Finally, I was promised one for my seventh birthday. The day came, and I was up nice and early looking all round for my bicycle with no sign of one anywhere! Then, I spotted a new picture on the mantelpiece in the sitting room – it was a beautiful bicycle! I burst into tears. I guess I was too young for a joke. I shall never forget the feeling of being betrayed. When Marta and Nanna found me and realized what had happened, I was quickly led to the place where my beautiful real bicycle was hidden. It was in the corner behind the sofa under a white sheet. The impact on me that day was such that I have always been very hesitant to tease or to play jokes on children. Since I could already ride an adult bicycle without sitting on the seat, it did not take me long to get outside and enjoy the new one. However, I remember the impact of that "joke" to this day.

Each summer we left Farnley for several months and went to the southwest of Ireland where the Armitage family owned a beautiful island called Dinish. Dinish was situated about six miles west of the small town of Kenmare near the south bank of Kenmare River. We all looked forward to our summers at Dinish. We often had many guests staying there with us, and they were all required to be in attendance at Morning Prayers. Some of these guests were missionaries who shared about their work in far off lands. Several were from China. I remember sitting on the windowsill, quite close to where Marta was playing the piano, and singing from the depths of my heart:

Follow, follow, I would follow Jesus,

Anywhere, everywhere, I would follow on.

Follow, follow, I would follow Jesus,

Ev'rywhere He leads me I would follow on.

Grandpa Armitage would read from his great big Bible, and then he or one of the guests would pray. I reveled in it all. Did I realize then that I would be following Jesus to the farthest corners of China in years to come? Perhaps deep down I did.

During the summer months when we were at Dinish Island, we would always go to church by boat. However wet, however stormy, Sunday mornings were church time. We had to go to the north side of Kenmare River. My recollection is that it took a good half-hour in the motorboat. I loved to sit up in the front of the boat. I got lots of spray in my face, but I could see the waves coming and feel the bumps as we went over the crest of the wave. Then we had to walk at least five minutes . . . maybe longer . . . it has been a long time since I took that walk! As we approached this little church a hushed awe came over us all. I loved to sit by Betty Armitage, Marta's youngest sister, because I sensed in her a nearness to God. Some years later, when I was twelve, it was Betty who paid for me to go to a Christian camp where I understood for the first time the real meaning of being a Christian.

Another deep impression from my "Dinish Days" is the house itself. It was a bungalow with a long winding passage going from one end to the other. The guestrooms were on either side of this passageway which started at the back of the building, went past the master bedroom where Granny and Grandpa Armitage slept, and then into the main hallway and to the official front door. From there you could look out over the beautiful lawn and see the ocean.

From the main hall you could go straight ahead into a large dining room and on to the smoking room, or you could go round the corner to the left and into the kitchen where the cooks were always making the most delicious soda bread. We children were not allowed to go into the kitchen except with special permission.

Back to those long corridors. Why do I remember them? All along both sides of the walls there were beautifully written and framed Bible verses. I would read them over and over again. I expect that is where I started to memorize the Word and meditate on it, although no one ever told me that I should. The Word of God became precious to me even before I really understood why. Grandpa Armitage often encouraged us children to love and reverence God's Word.

Other memories from Dinish days include swimming to the mainland. We were not allowed to try this until we had proven ourselves with various tests. I do not remember what they all were, but I worked hard to be the youngest person to make the swim. A dingy always rowed beside us in case we got into difficulties.

Opposite the southern side of Dinish there was a mountain called Coran. We would often challenge visitors to a race up Coran and then back down. I had several sprained ankles as a result of trying to break records on the race down.

Southern Ireland is beautiful. Killarney, well known for its lakes, was another favorite stomping ground. It was quite a long drive, so we often took a picnic lunch and spent a whole day sightseeing when we went. The mountains, covered with huge trees, came right down into the lakes. Sometimes there were waterfalls cascading down through the trees into the lakes. My recollection is that we were never allowed to swim there as it was considered too dangerous.

Of course, those wonderful long summer holidays in southern Ireland had to come to an end, and it was back to Farnley Hall, and back to driving to school with Alfred. But then, when I was eight years old, everything changed.

My father, who had been in and out of a mental hospital for many years after his unsuccessful attempt to settle in New Zealand, was again able to hold a job. He and my mother set up house together once more. At this point, I was sent back to my parents. This was a difficult time for all of us. Marta was like a mother to me, and I was so used to her and Nanna that I did not want to live with my parents. Finally the Armitage family paid for me to start at a small boarding school called St.Christopher's in Bexhill on Sea. This alleviated the situation considerably, because I enjoyed the school and only went home for brief periods at a time.

As soon as I was twelve years old, I started going to Christian camps. It was at the first of these, in the summer of 1936, I gave my life to the Lord. I remember vividly being asked to read a few verses out loud in an evening meeting. I was scared stiff, but made my decision then to follow the Lord at any cost—even if I risked making a fool of myself. So for me, becoming a Christian was not going forward at a meeting or praying a special prayer. It was the culmination of those years of hearing and seeing the Word of God with the Armitage family.

After I became a Christian, my life quickly changed. One little incident sticks with me. When I returned home from school one weekend, my father produced a letter that I had sent home, and he asked me if I had written it. Every Sunday afternoon we were forced to write home before being allowed to play outside. I had written the letter, but had a friend help me with the spelling. There was not one single spelling mistake, and this was unheard of from me! I was not known for honesty, but that day I told my parents that I'd had help with the spelling, and they realized that my becoming a Christian really had made a difference in my life. The Bible tells us, "If anyone is in Christ he is a new creation, old things have passed away, all things have become new" (2 Corinthians 5:17). I can't say that from then on I never told another lie, but every time I did lie, the Holy Spirit would quickly convict me and I would have to deal with it before peace returned to my heart.

Not long after that I had to leave St. Christopher's and move on to St. Margaret's, Bushey for my high school days. I was moving closer to my lifetime dream.

As the years went by and World War II began, most of us were facing conscription into one of the Armed Forces. As one accepted for Nursing School at a large London hospital (St. Bartholomew's or "Barts") I was encouraged to continue towards the career I had chosen. All medical and nursing students were held to their training because of the great need for doctors and nurses to care for the wounded and to help at the front lines.

So, in September 1942, I entered Barts' Preliminary Training School. As a nurse in training I wasn't just being trained medically, but also spiritually. I immediately lined myself up with the Barts Christian Union, which had a weekly meeting as well as small prayer groups and Bible studies. After two months at the Preliminary Training School, I was sent to Hill End (the sector hospital at St. Albans, just north of London). A major part of Barts had been evacuated there because of all the bombing in London at that time.

Within six months of transferring to Hill End, the Lord sent my future life partner to join us in the Christian Union. Donald was a medical student who had been evacuated from Barts in London up to Cambridge University because of the bombing. Having finished his pre-medical exams, he came to Hill End to start his time in the hospital wards. We met in the Christian Union within days of his arrival.

Donald used to enjoy saying to people who asked him about his background and nationality, "They call me 'White Chinese' because I was born in China." According to his passport, he was born on July 18, 1923 in Thai Yong (Da Yang), Southern China. His parents were on holiday in the mountains where they shared a small summer cottage. Donald's birth certificate, however, says he was born in Wu Jing Fu. This is a small town at the foot of the mountains where his father worked in the English Presbyterian Mission hospital. To add to the confusion about his background and nationality, Donald's parents were both pure Scottish, and Donald was proud to call himself a Scot in the appropriate situations. Despite all this, when we applied for our green cards to retire in the United States, he was still considered "White Chinese."

It was not long after Donald had arrived at Hill End that we discovered that we were both there because we believed that God had called us to China. Our hearts were being drawn ever closer to the Lord, and closer to each other. We never discussed what we would do after we were married, only how we would get to China. We knew we had to wait until the war was over. We also knew that the conventional way of going to China with a missionary society was not open to us because of Donald's life-long chronic asthmatic condition. There was, however, a certainty in our hearts that God planned to take us there, in His time, and in His way, and we rejoiced in this assurance and waited.

I finished my training at the end of 1945, and Donald finished his very early in May 1946. We were married at St. Martins-in-the-Fields on May 10th, having fulfilled our promise to my parents that we would not get married until we had both finished our training.

CHAPTER 2

LIVING IN THE EAST END
May 10, 1946 to October 10, 1948

"Delight yourself in the Lord and He will give you the desires of your heart."
Psalm 37:4

The Rev. Graham Hobson read Proverbs 3:5-6 at our wedding: "Trust in the Lord with *all* your heart, and lean *not* to your own understanding. In *all* your ways acknowledge Him, and He *shall* direct your paths." These verses immediately became applicable to our situation.

Our Irish honeymoon was my opportunity to introduce Donald to many of my childhood haunts. We spent most of our time at Dinish Island, where the Sullivans thoroughly spoiled us with homemade soda bread, freshly churned butter, a huge baked ham, and all the luscious things we had not seen or tasted during the war years.

We went to Ireland knowing we were to return to a locum practice in the southwest of England. After that, Donald did not have a job. During our honeymoon we received a letter from the Inter-varsity Christian Fellowship headquarters telling us of doctors in the dock area of the East End of London who were wanting a young Christian doctor as "an assistant with view to partnership." That sounded great, BUT we were headed for China. Donald wrote back that he would be glad to come for an interview with a view to being an assistant for a while, BUT that we were headed for China as soon as the door opened. We learned later that they never expected us to go to China.

Donald was accepted, and shortly after we had finished the locum we moved to Bermondsey, southeast London. We moved in with the senior partner and his wife for about nine months, and then after our first boy, Andrew Colin, was born, we moved in with another doctor who asked us to keep house for him. This house was attached to one of the two medical offices and was therefore very convenient for Donald in his medical work. We had learned a very important lesson. When we trust in the Lord and do not try to figure things out for ourselves, choosing to acknowledge Him in everything, His promise is that He will direct our paths. How wonderfully He had provided for us. We remained in this practice for just over two years.

We had not been living with Dr. Mumford very long when the letter from China that was going to change our lives arrived on our doorstep. That morning, as soon as Donald and I saw the envelope and stamps from China, we looked at each other and said, "This is our way to China." The Lord put such a certainty into our hearts that when we opened the letter and saw it was all written in Chinese, we had no doubts that He had opened the door. We had to wait a few days until we saw one of our Chinese friends at church and asked her to read it and translate it for us. As Donald handed her the letter he said, "This is our way to China." As she read it we watched her face, then she looked at us and said, "Are you sure?" We assured her we were. Then she told us that the letter was from the mayor of a small town in west China called Beipei. He was asking us to go and work in his newly built municipal hospital. He wanted us to come as soon as we could. He understood that we were Christians and said we would be free to share our faith. He would provide accommodation for us. Donald would be paid a salary of ten sacks of rice a month.

Although at that time everyone, including us, wondered what we would do with ten sacks of rice each month, after we arrived in Beipei that question was quickly answered. Rice was the staple currency, and money was literally halving in value overnight. The letter continued to tell us that we would need to get ourselves to Shanghai, then the mayor's brother, who was the head of the Min Sheng Shipping Company, would look after us and see that we got up the Yangtze River to Chongqing. They would meet us there and take us on to Beipei, about half a day's journey by bus. We were overjoyed. Our friends and family thought we were crazy, but we were sure the Lord was saying to us, "Do not lean to your own understanding, don't try and figure it out yourselves, just trust Me totally and completely; I will direct you."

You may be wondering how the mayor of Beipei had our names and address. During the war, while Donald and I were both in medical training, we had occasion to visit missionary friends staying at the South Africa General Mission (S.A.G.M.) headquarters in south London. While there, we were introduced to an elderly couple who had been serving the Lord in west China with the Church Missionary Society, and who just "happened" to be staying in the S.A.G.M. headquarters at the time we visited our friends. Archdeacon and Mrs. Donnithorne were unable to return to Sichuan during the war. They took our names and address because we shared with them our desire to go to China when we had finished our training at Barts. After the war ended, the Donnithornes returned to west China. One day, the mayor of Beipei invited them to a feast. Often in China this means that the one inviting you wants a favor. In this case, at the end of the meal the mayor asked, "Do you know a British or American doctor who would come and work in the new municipal hospital here in Beipei?" The Donnithornes promised to get our names and address to him, and you know the rest of the story! Donald wrote to the mayor accepting the invitation, and we told Dr. Gillison and Dr. Mumford that we would be leaving for China in the spring of 1948.

Our time in Bermondsey had been very helpful to Donald in getting somewhat established in general medical practice before leaving for China. But, it also was most profitable spiritually as we got tied in as a family at our local church, the Honor Oak Christian Fellowship Center (H.O.) in Forest Hill, southeast London. We were able to drive from our home in Bermondsey to the church in just over ten minutes, and one or the other of us would be at every service. In those days we had Sunday services both mornings and evenings, and prayer meetings on Tuesday and Saturday, as well as Bible study on Thursday. We had excellent Bible teaching from T. Austin-Sparks and others, which stood us in such good stead when we were faced with challenging situations in the years ahead. Truly the Word became "a lamp to our feet and a light to our path" (Psalm 119:105).

We have always been very grateful for the grounding in the Word of God that we were given throughout the war years and then at H.O. We could have been anywhere in the British Isles, but the Lord in His infinite wisdom and perfect planning took us to this work in Bermondsey, so close to H.O. He tied us into a fellowship that He knew was already interested in China and had actually had Watchman Nee visiting with them just prior to World War II. Honor Oak Fellowship also had several missionaries who had served many years in China. We were surrounded by people who were praying for China, and were genuinely interested in seeing others go to serve the Lord in that land.

I had been baptized at H.O. while I was in nurses' training during the war years. Donald had been confirmed while at Monkton, and this had meant much to him. He felt it had been the testimony to the outside world that baptism is meant to be. For a number of years this caused him to feel he did not need to be baptized. However, he finally decided that the Lord was telling him he needed to be baptized as an example for those we would be teaching in China. It was a happy day when this matter was settled in Donald's heart, and he knew the way the Lord was leading him. It was a true step of obedience.

While we were living in Bermondsey, my father died suddenly in November 1947. My parents were living on a boat moored alongside the wharf near Cannon Street railway station. However, the night Dad was taken sick they were actually spending time at our home while the boat was being repaired. My brother, Neil, was away at boarding school. After father's death the boat was sold and my mother and brother came to live with us until the time we left for China. It was good that we were still around and able to support my mother through her time of loss.

The Lord was truly preparing us during our early years of life together. We felt like I should attend Honor Oak's Bible school known as "West Watch." Arrangements were made for Andrew to be cared for by a friend during the day, as I would be away Monday to Friday. This lasted exactly ten days. Shortly after arriving at West Watch, I started to have "morning sickness" and realized our second child was on the way. By the end of the second week it became quite evident I was not going to be able to cope, so when I went home for the next weekend, I stayed home. Those next few weeks I spent most of my time in bed very nauseated. It was during that time that my father died, and my mother really needed me at home. Having to give up Bible school was sad and really disappointing, but the Lord knew what was best, and it became, as so often is the case, an example of all things working together for good for those who love God. Because of this second pregnancy, we wrote to the Mayor and the Donnithornes saying we felt we should delay our leaving for China until October. We would leave when our baby was three months old. Peter Robin was born in early July.

During this delay we were also to meet Esther Cui, who had been sent to London Bible College by the Donnithornes. It was so good to be able to talk to someone actually from Beipei and learn more about the Donnithornes and the work of the West China Evangelistic Band, which they had been instrumental in starting. This was another instance of all things working together for good for those who love the Lord.

After working two years in this Christian medical practice, we moved in August 1948 to a house that belonged to H.O., which the church made available to us for our last couple of months in England. My mother moved with us and was a tremendous help in cooking and caring for Andrew and Robin while Donald and I were packing and doing all the last-minute odd jobs before leaving England. There was a lot to do. After all, we planned to be gone for about seven years. Robin was only a month old when we moved down to Forest Hill. We were within walking distance of the church, and we were able to get to know many of the fellowship considerably better during those last two months. The prayer support they gave us during our long trip to China has continued to this day. Throughout the years, we have constantly thanked God for a praying church behind us.

CHAPTER 3

SLOW BOAT TO CHINA
Oct.10, 1948 to Jan.1, 1949

**"The Lord will watch over your coming and going both
now and forevermore."
Psalm 121:8**

On the night of October 9, 1948, Euston railway station in
north London saw a large group of church friends and others,
including my mother, Hazel Harding, gather to sing and pray us
on our way. This was the beginning of our seventeen-week journey to Beipei, Sichuan in West China.

We arrived in Glasgow at around 6.a.m. and were given a
warm welcome by a group of Christian friends. Then we were
taken to one of their homes. This was a Sunday morning, and
what a joy to spend our last few hours on British soil worshipping with them. We were reminded once again that we were
going forth in His Name, in the wonderful Name of Jesus.

Soon after lunch it was time to be taken to the docks. The
"Rhexenor" was a small cargo vessel that took only twelve passengers. Our passage was booked from Glasgow to Shanghai,
but the route was basically unknown. We had however been told
to get American visas since we would be going across the Atlantic and not through the Mediterranean and Suez Canal as origi-

nally expected.

The Lord was taking care of us from the start. Donald's mother turned up ten minutes before we had to board the ship, and our luggage that had been mislaid between Carlisle and Glasgow was found and arrived just in time. We learned much later that the LMS (London, Midland and Scotland) railway officials had been urged into feverish activity on account of Donald being "an important member of the Ministry of Health." We could not help smiling at the interesting way the Lord intervened to see to it that our luggage was all on board!

One week of rather stormy weather across the Atlantic, a lot of sea-sickness, and not much opportunity to get to know the few other passengers saw us entering the St. Lawrence river with approximately 600 miles to go from the estuary to Montreal. The autumn coloring on the south side of the estuary touched by snow overnight was beautiful.

Donald's daily diary records on that first Sunday, "Today has been very much like every other day, except that nearly everyone had their tidy clothes on! This was the only way that Sunday was celebrated!" So began a consciousness in our spirits of an important question: what in our background was just tradition, and what was really scriptural principle that we should be following? Little did we realize how often this question would arise in the days and years ahead.

Andrew felt very confined again on board ship after two days exploring Montreal. Donald's diary comments, "He still shows more interest in the things which he is not allowed to do than in his toys, and we spend our time rescuing the knitting and books of other passengers from his grasp." The diary goes on to say, "Psalm 109:4b, 'I give myself to prayer,' has been the best thought for today and is very applicable to our time on board."

So the days moved on. We zigzagged north and south across the East Coast to pick up cargo in the right order to accommodate being unloaded in the Far East. While in New York for several days, we were taken by retired China missionaries to stay in their home. They had been notified by the leaders of our church in London that we would be on this ship. On our last day with them, we enjoyed the Sunday morning worship service in their home, and we met a number of other believers. After lunch, it was time for us to be taken back to the ship. On the way, we had our next "Sunday" challenge, a stop to eat ice cream! We never bought anything on a Sunday except in a real emergency, especially something we considered an unnecessary luxury! Here was the next tradition we had to weigh carefully against Scripture.

Meanwhile, the news from China was not good. Both the American and British civilians had been asked to leave Shanghai and Nanking, and, sadly, in England, they were still more interested in the birth of Prince Charles than in a country as far away as China.

Once safely through the Panama Canal, we faced 4000 miles heading north to Vancouver, because the Los Angeles and San Francisco ports where we were supposed to be stopping were on strike. We had to stay in Vancouver for ten days because of continuous heavy rain. The sacks of flour to be loaded had to be protected. We searched the telephone directory looking for churches and praying we'd be able to get in touch with some Christians, but we didn't have much luck. Finally, when we were about to sail, four missionaries with the China Inland Mission (C.I.M.) got on board along with two little boys just steps older than Andrew and Robin. We had never thought of finding C.I.M. headquarters in Vancouver; they belonged to England in our thinking!

While in Vancouver, we did manage to contact some distant Dale cousins, and we went out with them for a couple of meals. It was good to talk of the family, and it was a nice break on our long journey. These cousins told us that Donald and his parents had been in their home in 1928 on the way back to England, but he did not remember anything of that journey.

On December 1st, we were finally heading out of Vancouver harbor due west across the Pacific. The weather got worse and worse. The notes in our diary from December 4th tell of the Lord's protection in the midst of the storm:

> It looks as though the sea has no intention of subsiding and now, although there is not so much roll, the boat is pitching badly. We had one scare in the night when the roll got particularly bad. We woke to hear an awful crash. When we turned the light on we discovered that Robin and his carrycot had slipped off the chest of drawers. This

should not have been possible since there was a high rim around the upper edge of the chest of drawers to make it impossible for the cot to move. In such a storm nothing was impossible! Robin had been thrown out of the cot and was caught by his nightdress on the radiator faucet, while the carrycot had crashed on to the floor. He was somewhat startled to find himself hanging upside down swinging from the radiator, but he was totally unhurt. How thankful we were for the Lord's protection over him.

The following Sunday, December 5th, we were ready to start our Bible studies. We had already decided to study II Corinthians. It was great to have some real fellowship again. For the next two weeks we had Chinese lessons in the mornings with Frances Williamson while Jeanie Dougan kindly watched both our boys and the Lindbergs'. The Lord not only provided a teacher for the four of us during that time crossing the Pacific, but also a babysitter willing to watch all four little boys. Each day after lunch we had Bible study, and in the evenings we tried to do some "homework" for the next day's Chinese lesson. These days were busy days, but they were much enjoyed by all. One excitement was when a floating mine was sighted which came quite close to our ship but fortunately passed without hitting us. In those days after World War II, there were still quite a number of mines floating around in the Pacific.

It was so good to have other Christians on board. We all enjoyed the Bible studies, and by the second weekend we had permission to have a Sunday service in the lounge. On Friday evening we had a prayer meeting and also made final preparations for the service. The next day was Sunday, since we skipped Saturday altogether because of the date line. The service went well; about twenty people attended. Bob Lindberg led, Major Gibson prayed, the Chief Engineer read the lesson, and Donald gave a little talk on 1 John 1:5.

By the middle of December, Donald's diary mentions our boys again. Robin had started to enjoy eating potatoes and vegetables put through a sieve at midday and had already for some time been eating as much Farex (Pablum) as I allowed him. Because of this, Donald had to do some major searching for more Farex in our luggage in the hold. Andrew, meanwhile, was a bit rough with the other boys and certainly the master of any given situation. He had quite a shock one morning when he nearly fell through the railings onto the lower deck. Fortunately his reins held, and Donald was close at hand.

The weather finally improved, and we were averaging around 380 miles a day making good progress towards Manila in the Philippines. Meanwhile, our Chinese lessons continued. Donald's diary comments, "We are now on vocabulary six and this brings our total number of words to about 150. We are starting to get really well muddled since the same Chinese sound can mean many different things, and even when it has the same tone there are different meanings. It is hard to describe but even harder to learn!"

Sunday, December 19, we had an excellent morning service with all the old Christmas hymns. Unfortunately, no one except Donald and I knew the tune to "O little town of Bethlehem," so we sang a duet for the first verse and then sang other hymns. Bob Lindberg spoke from Isaiah on the names given to Christ before He was born. In the evening, we gathered for a little testimony meeting so that in the future we should all have a good foundation for praying for one another. Also, late in the evening, we received a cable from Mr. Simon Meek in Manila welcoming us and telling us he would be meeting us on Tuesday. Leaders from Honor Oak had contacted the Chinese Church in Manila where Brother Meek was one of the leading elders at Solar Street Assembly. Donald's diary describes our welcoming:

> As we woke on Tuesday morning, we were steaming into Manila Bay past Corregidor, the scene of McArthur's last bitter struggle against the Japanese. By noon we had finished with all the formalities, and the boat docked at about 1:30 p.m. As we were tying up, two powerful American cars pulled up alongside the boat, and a group of well-dressed Chinese gentlemen got out, obviously intent on meeting the boat. Their spotless white suits and whole demeanor gave us the impression of well-to-do businessmen. What was our surprise when one of them cupped his hands and called up to all the waiting passengers, "Is Dr. Dale on board?" They had come to meet us. It appeared that Mr. Meek was away in China

at that moment for health reasons, but the elders of his church had got together and decided to come en masse to meet us and invite us to stay at the chapel for a day or two.

After we had packed a few things together we drove off in one of the cars. When the elders heard that there were other missionaries on board, they also asked them to come for the evening meeting and a meal. We went first to the chapel and saw the room where we would be staying. It was on the ground floor, where two other families lived. The meeting hall was upstairs. We were then taken by car to see the new gospel radio station and the Bible Institute, which were both started by ex G.I s. At that time, the radio program was only four hours every evening in about four different languages, but they hoped soon to have short wave to cover the whole of the Far East. This was the beginning of the Far Eastern Broadcasting Company (FEBC) as we know it today. We met several of the Americans concerned with the running of this station and were much impressed with their utter dependence on the Lord and with the quality of the programs they put on the air. We then returned to the chapel, put the children to bed in our room and went out to a Chinese supper at the new YMCA. At this time, we met all the other elders and had our first experience of eating a real Chinese meal with our Chinese brothers and sisters and, of course, using chopsticks. When a large whole fish, head and all, was put on the table facing Donald, one dear brother dug out the fish's eye and put it in Donald's bowl. This was more than he could face; he picked it up and passed it on to the next brother beside him! Years later we learned that this was indeed the correct and polite thing to do, but at that moment it was rather an embarrassing situation. After the meal, we were taken back to the chapel for the evening meeting where we were asked to give short testimonies. They had to be interpreted. Dr. Huang, one of the leading elders, was well able to do this. This was our first introduction to a Chinese service, and we thoroughly enjoyed ourselves.

On Wednesday evening, Donald was asked to share concerning the work going on at Honor Oak. The Chinese Christians were all very interested in H.O. because it was our home church, and Brother Watchman Nee had visited it during his trip to England in the late 1930s. Those able to read English were also reading Austin-Spark's books and the "Witness and Testimony" magazine that was published once a month. Donald spoke for about three-quarters of an hour and then had to answer questions for at least another half-hour. Dr. Huang was again asked to interpret. We had enjoyed an excellent Chinese meal with him before the meeting. We appreciated so much the wonderful hospitality given to us because we were complete strangers to them.

The diary repeatedly refers to the fact that Andrew would not eat any of the Chinese food, but fortunately he was happy to sit on the floor and play with the chopsticks while everyone else feasted. We were back on board ship by Christmas Eve and had a happy but very hot Christmas Day with a children's party in the afternoon. It was strange to us to have no Christmas Day morning service. Instead we gathered in the Lindberg's cabin and opened presents. A number of parcels from England had been sent to Manila as well as the many gifts that the Chinese brothers and sisters had showered upon us. Finally, we sat outside on the deck and listened to the B.B.C. until it was time for King George VI's Christmas speech to the nation. After the speech, it was to bed at midnight once again.

The following day was Sunday, and Donald was to speak at the Chinese church in the morning. Bob Lindberg was to speak in the evening. We all spent the afternoon together with the church folk who were keen to get lots of photos of all of us. We too were happy for the opportunity to get some pictures of them. Years later we had further touches with these dear brothers and sisters in Manila; some visited us in Taiwan, and we saw others when we had another occasion to visit the Philippines.

We left Manila early on Tuesday morning at which time the Captain told us he still was not sure if he could go to Shanghai because of the political situation. He might have to leave us all in Hong Kong. The communist troops were expected to take Shanghai at any moment. In the end, the Captain took us in to Shanghai early on January 1st, 1949. He got all of us unloaded as quickly as possible, and he was away well before nightfall. The main excitement of the day was that Andrew threw the football he had been given for Christmas into the sea and proceeded to try and follow it himself. He was only saved by the timely intervention of a member of the crew. That evening, Miss Williamson spoke to the Lindberg's and Donald and I concerning the special temptations befalling missionaries. She and Jeanie Dougan were an incredible blessing to us on this trip. It was certainly of the Lord that we all sailed from Vancouver to Shanghai together. We not only learned a tiny bit of the Chinese language before arriving in China, but, perhaps far more important, we received much wise advice.

New Year's Eve was spent anchored at the mouth of the Yangtze since the dense fog the night before had slowed us up considerably. By the time the pilot was able to get aboard, it was too late to go into Shanghai that evening. Early morning January 1, 1949 we finally anchored at Holt's wharf. We stayed on board with those who had come to meet us until our luggage was all safely in the launch to be delivered to the customs shed. Mr. Tan, of the Ming Seng Shipping Company, then took us to the customs wharf on the famous Shanghai Bund.

It was twelve weeks to the day since we sailed down the Clyde, away from the British Isles, on a very wet Sunday afternoon—we had finally arrived on Chinese soil.

Our hearts were truly rejoicing, "Jesus led us all the way."

CHAPTER 4

SHANGHAI
January 1949

"The Lord will fulfill His purpose for me."
Psalm 138:8

NEW YEARS DAY, 1949 – Early morning the quarantine and immigration officials came on board, and by 11:30 a.m., we were alongside Holt's Wharf. We were met by three Chinese gentlemen. Mr. Tan, was making all arrangements for us while we were in Shanghai. Dr. Wang was to travel to Beipei by river steamer with us. A friend of Dr. Wang's also joined the group to help in any way he could. They all stayed aboard until our luggage had been put onto a launch; then we accompanied them in their launch, which belonged to the Min Sheng Shipping Company. We landed on the Shanghai Bund, an impressive waterfront where ships from around the world were anchored. All our baggage, except for the crates, went through the customs right away. The crates were detained along with our wireless radio, for which we needed a license, and our medical drugs, which had to be assessed. After these matters were resolved, we were driven by car (again provided freely by the shipping company) to the China Inland Mission (C.I.M.) headquarters. Here, we were shown to our room, which was large and comfortable after the cramped quarters of the ship's cabin. There were two beds, a cot for Andrew, and some room to temporarily unpack our cases. After supper, we got Andrew and Robin ready for bed. Donald and I were tired as well, but we were also thrilled to be enjoying our first night as a family on Chinese soil. We were a bit overwhelmed by the fact we were actually in China. It was still hard to believe!

The next day was Sunday. We went to an English service at the Free Christian Church, a protégé church of the C.I.M. We spent the rest of the day settling into our room. We were in a state of awe and shock those first few days in Shanghai, which was the third largest city in the world at that time. The streets were crowded with vehicles of every description, from new American cars to rickshaws.

Donald spent most of the next day down at the customs. The Min Sheng Shipping Company provided one of their most senior officials, an expert in customs formalities, to accompany him since it was essential that he had someone to interpret. Later in the afternoon of January 5th, they came across an Englishman who was high up in the customs office and able to hurry things up considerably. Many more visits were necessary to actually get everything cleared. A radio license had to be obtained, and the drugs we brought had to be cleared—despite the fact that Donald was a medical doctor, and quite a bit of what we had was for his own prophylactic use. We were grateful that his asthma had been under good control all throughout our long journey. The duty on everything had to be assessed and, to our great relief, was only about one quarter of the expected cost. In retrospect, we realized we had brought far more supplies than were essential, but at the time it had seemed sensible to make use of a certain post-war privilege.

Knowing long before we got married that we would be going to China, we asked people to give us money rather than material goods for wedding presents. We saved this money to use when we knew how and where we would be going. At this time, the late 1940s, many British goods were "for export only." By mid-1947, when we knew we would be going to Sichuan, we began to look into the possibility of buying from the export market. Things were cheaper and often of better quality when they were bought that way. The disadvantage was that all we bought had to be sent straight to the ship and could not be looked at until we were more than twelve miles from land. Of course, everything was crated, and we had no intention of opening the crates until we got to Shanghai and had to open them for the customs. This is how we bought brand new bicycles, bed linens, blankets, camp cots, sleeping bags, a twelve-piece dinner service, and many other things. Little did we know, all of this would never get to Beipei, and most of it would never even be used by us. That story will have to come a bit later. Sufficient to say that the Lord's ways truly are not our ways, but they are wonderful.

During our time in Shanghai, we met Gladys Aylward and Mrs. Mary Twinem who were sharing a room next door to ours, at the C.I.M. headquarters. Mrs. Twinem was to become Madam Chiang Kai-shek's personal English-speaking secretary, and she would help Madam in this capacity for many years while they all lived in Taiwan. Miss Aylward later became well known around the world as "The Small Woman," or "The London Sparrow" as one book written about her was titled. One evening, Gladys and Mary offered to watch our boys sleep while we went off to spend the evening with a number of other young couples. When we returned, there was no sign of our baby, Robin. We soon found him having a great time entertaining his two "baby-sitters" and enjoying being the center of attention. Twelve years later, Robin and I spent some time with Mrs. Twinem and Miss Aylward in Taiwan, and we all had a good laugh together about them absconding with our baby. By then, Mrs. Twinem was working with Madam Chiang Kai-shek, and she had become well known and much appreciated by the rest of the foreign community. Gladys also had arrived in Taiwan and was about to open an orphanage in Tien Mu, a suburb of Taipei.

The day finally came when our passports were endorsed for Sichuan, and another milestone was crossed. In those days, one could not move from one province to another without official permission, which was not always easy to obtain. Going up the Yangtze River to Chongqing, we would go through Anhui and Hubei provinces before reaching Sichuan.

It was a special blessing to be able to see Miss Joy Betteridge while we were in Shanhai. She was also from the Honor Oak Christian Fellowship in south London. Joy worked with a Chinese church that was part of the Watchman Nee group, known in the western world as the "Little Flock." This fellowship was doing a tremendous work amongst the students at that time, and over one hundred had been baptized just the week before. Miss Betteridge was in Shanghai at the time we arrived, and she came over to the C.I.M. headquarters to visit us. She took us out to lunch one day with a young Chinese couple, who worked with her in the church and spoke English quite well. After lunch, two other sisters from the church joined us. Altogether it was a lovely time of fellowship and a real treat to be with them all.

Being able to attend a meeting where Gladys Aylward spoke was another highlight of our time in Shanghai. She shared about getting away from the Japanese army with over a hundred orphan children for whom she had been caring. She led them over the mountains to safety in an orphanage in Xian. Not one child was lost, even though the youngest ones were only four and five years old. The older children helped carry these little ones when they got too tired to walk further or their feet were too sore and their shoes worn out. God's miraculous provisions of transportation, food, and shelter are recorded in the story of her life in the series "Heroes of the Faith." Gladys also helped us a number of times when either Donald or I needed to go out shopping. She would direct us and also come along as our interpreter.

Now that we had our passports, it was time for the actual trip to Sichuan. The journey was not an easy one. We were frequently given a date when we should be ready to get onto the river steamer headed for Chongqing only to have it changed. Once we were told the ship needed repairs. Another time the communist armies had reached the north bank of the river and were shooting at any boats trying to go upstream. When, finally, on January 19th or 20th, our luggage was released from customs, we were told that all the Min Sheng Passenger ships sailing upriver had been cancelled because of the political situation. This meant we must consider alternative transportation. One possibility was flying. Our luggage would have to follow in a landing craft as freight. Another possibility was to have me and the children fly while Donald and Dr Wang would accompany the luggage on the landing craft. In the end, we all flew on the Lutheran mission plane known as the "St. Paul." This was the only plane that would take enough of our luggage, and since no one could guarantee when the rest of our crates would follow, we felt we had to try and take quite a bit with us.

January 21st, 1949, Generalissimo Chiang Kai-shek resigned from the presidency, and the political situation became even more uncertain. No one knew if the Nationalists and the Communists would try to come to some sort of agreement, and, with Chinese New Year only a week away, nothing tangible could be arranged immediately. Finally, on Friday, February 4th, the great day arrived. The St. Paul took us all (together with 500 lbs. of baggage, including our pram and pushchair) to Chongqing in only six hours. What a blessing from the Lord—six hours of flight rather than two to three weeks on an extremely primitive river steamer. We were very thankful to have reached Sichuan and to be so close to our destination. The St. Paul landed on a small island in the middle of the river, where a grass strip served as a runway when the water was low enough. The business manager of the C.I.M. and an English-speaking representative of the shipping company met us. They took us to the C.I.M. headquarters to spend the night. The following day, both the mayor of Beipei and the superintendent of the hospital arrived to greet us and to tell us that everything was prepared for us to travel on to Beipei by bus the following day.

Sunday, February 6th, 1949, we arrived at our longed-for destination. But even that last day of travelling had its adventures. After a lot of haggling with the coolies over the price to be paid to get our luggage to the bus, we finally got to the so-called "bus station." There were two more mishaps before we actually got onto the bus. First, the bus had a flat tire. Then, an attendant put water into the gas tank instead of gas. An hour and a half later, we started getting onto the bus—an adventure in itself. The wooden seats stretched right across the bus, so those sitting in the back had to climb over the seats. When everyone else had climbed in, we were given two seats in the front. I was next to the driver with Robin on my lap. Donald was squashed behind the driver with Andrew. The mayor and the hospital superintendent sat beside Donald.

The road from Chongqing to Beipei was pretty. It was also quite an engineering feat with many hairpin bends, and it rose to at least one and a half thousand feet in a couple of places. It was dark when we arrived, but we found ourselves on a smooth tarmac road, lined with trees and lit by dim electric lights. We were taken to the local hotel for supper with the mayor and his wife. We also met Archdeacon and Mrs. Donnithorne and David Day, who were busy with a tent campaign that had been running over the Chinese New Year. Taken to our temporary quarters where our luggage had already been carried, we found that we had been given five rooms on the lower floor of one of the biggest houses in Beipei until such time as a new house could be built. This was very convenient since we were near to the Donnithornes, and also to the clinic where Donald was to go each morning. It only remained for us, at the end of this long journey, to record once again how conscious we had been all along the way of God's help in answer to the faithful prayers of many of His children. We gave Him all the glory; great things had He done.

CHAPTER 5

BEIPEI AT LAST
February 6th to mid-May 1949

"In everything give thanks."
I Thessalonians 5:18

We said to each other that first night in Beipei, "How wonderful to be where we hope to stay at least seven years – no more travelling." Little did we know, in three and a half months we would find ourselves in Hong Kong. The Lord's ways were certainly not our ways, nor His thoughts our thoughts. One week after we arrived in Beipei, Donald made a final entry in the notebook that he had faithfully kept since the day we left the United Kingdom: "We are beginning to settle in, but finding it difficult on account of having to wait for most of our luggage to arrive from Shanghai. But the Lord has provided wonderfully in every way, and the friends of the West China Evangelistic Band (W.C.E.B.) have supplied everything we could possibly need until such time as our luggage arrives."

Our daily routine soon seemed to fall into place. Donald spent most mornings at the hospital while I was with the children. We had our main meal at noon with the Donnithornes. This gave us daily contact with them and with some of the church folk from whom we quickly began to learn some Chinese customs. We also got to enjoy some homemade Chinese food. We began regular language lessons and soon realized it would be a life-long project! But we pressed on, and each new little phrase we could say was a cause for rejoicing. What we had learned while on the boat was proving very useful.

Beipei was quite a unique place in the spring of 1949. The mayor's older brother, who was head of the Min Sheng shipping company, was working with his younger brother to modernize the city of Beipei. The older brother was supplying most of the funds, and the younger was overseeing such improvements as tarmac roads, street lighting, and clean markets with properly covered food. From this background, the mayor had requested the Donnithornes to recommend a medical doctor who would come and work in the new municipal hospital. The mayor thought this would add considerable prestige to his modernization project. He did not understand how his offer of ten sacks of rice a month as Donald's salary was, in fact, the Lord's wonderful provision for our family. Paper money finally became worthless, and everything switched to silver dollars shortly before we flew out to Hong Kong in May 1949. Rice remained a stable currency.

Before we arrived, Mrs. Donnithorne found a woman who was willing to help us. We were told to pay her the equivalent of one US dollar per month. I am sure she must have helped sweep the floors and keep our home somewhat clean, but the things that stand out in my mind more than fifty years later are threefold. She would scrub our clothes on a wooden board in cold water. I wondered how the clothes would ever get clean, or how many holes would be found in them after just one washing! They all seemed to survive. I remember her putting peanuts between two huge stones and grinding them until something that resembled peanut butter oozed out from between the stones. Watching our lady scraping it up and putting it into a container cured me for life of ever wanting to eat peanut butter. Donald and Andrew on the other hand were glad to have something to put on their rather hard and dry homemade bread. Perhaps the most horrific of all was the "getting your sugar clean" performance. The sugar was put into a container resembling a saucepan and brought to the boil over an open charcoal fire. Our dear lady never stopped stirring. When it came to a boil, she proceeded to scrape the scum off the top with her wooden spoon and throw it away. This was done several times. When most of the dirt was scraped off, the boiling caldron was removed from the fire, and our friend had to continue to stir until the sugar crystallized once more. I don't remember exactly how long this process took, but I am sure it was at least one whole morning, maybe longer still. Since everyone in our family had rather a sweet tooth, this procedure went on at least once a week. How very grateful we were for our dear helper; she was certainly worth far more to us than the one US dollar a month we paid her. Forty six years later, in September 1995, when Donald and I were able to visit the church in Beipei once more, this dear soul walked many miles to come and see us and tell us that now she too knew and loved the Lord as we did. What a blessing!

The West China Evangelistic Band's Protestant church was small but active. Donald and I went regularly to the meetings there on Sundays, and at least one evening each week. Although we were unable to understand anything to begin with, we really enjoyed the fellowship and quickly began to feel right at home with them all. Esther Cui, whom we had originally met in London in 1947, was able to translate for us so we were able to participate as well as get the gist of what was going on. Everyone loved our two little boys, and the children soon got used to being picked up and cuddled by many different people. We had no shortage of baby-sitters, even when the boys were ill.

Almost immediately after we arrived in China, Andrew had an acute attack of tonsillitis from which he never really recovered. He was in bed practically the entire time we were in Sichuan. Only a week or two later, Robin had pneumonia, and he too ran a continuous fever from then on. Donald was afraid they might have picked up tuberculosis, so he sent an SOS to a doctor friend in London to ask him to send us TB patches. The patches arrived in due course, and both of the children turned out to be TB negative. Because of their continuous fevers, we decided that we should take both children to the Canadian Mission Hospital in Chongqing. We left Beipei by river steamer at the end of April and went down the Jialing River to Chongqing.

The mission hospital was on the south bank of the Yangtze. It was high above the river, and we were carried up to it in two rickshaws, Donald with Andrew on his lap and Robin strapped onto my lap. Coolies ran beside us with our luggage. We felt sorry for the men carrying us up such a steep and rough pathway. We were totally amazed at how sure-footed they were. Not one of them stumbled the whole way up. We would have had a hard time walking up it by ourselves, not to mention with sick children and luggage to carry. Members of the Canadian Presbyterian Mission greeted us when we finally reached the top. We were given comfortable quarters, and tests were started right away to try and ascertain what was causing the continuous fevers that both Andrew and Robin were experiencing. Nothing of any significance was found, but it was obvious that neither of the boys were up to par.

Finally, the sad decision was made that Donald would go back to Beipei, pack up the few possessions we had there and say our good-byes. By this time, our friends in Beipei had heard that the communist troops had crossed the border into Sichuan Province, and they advised Donald to leave because of the political turmoil. I would stay with the boys at the hospital until Donald returned. Then we would all fly out to Hong Kong and hospitalize the children again to see what the doctors could find out.

Meanwhile, the luggage that we had left in Shanghai was put on a boat and brought up to Chongqing. The communist troops had been pushed back from the north bank of the Yangtze near

Nanjing, the shooting had temporarily stopped, and everything was safely put into a storage place. None of it had ever been sent on to Beipei. What a blessing that was! Instead, when Donald returned to Chongqing, he was able to arrange for all our luggage to be moved to an empty room at the Bible Society. When it arrived, he unpacked it and sold what he could. Our brand new bicycles, and the beautiful, unused, warm woolen blankets and other linens sold immediately. The rest was packed up and later moved to one of the mission compounds. We told them to use anything they could and distribute the rest of it to those who could use it, as it was no good leaving things in boxes. We later learned that our twelve-piece dinner service and coffee set were used by the China Inland Mission (C.I.M.) language school for a couple of years. It was later divided into two six-piece dinner sets for two married couples. The coffee set went to a third couple, who took them off to Australia. So much for our wedding presents, most of which we never used, and I never even saw! It reminds me of what we were told in Shanghai while we stayed at the C.I.M. headquarters, "You are not considered real China missionaries until you have lost at least one child, and all your possessions three times."

Shortly after exchanging most of our possessions for silver dollars, we were once again able to arrange a flight on the St. Paul, this time to Canton. We took off from the same strip of grass in the middle of the river in Chongqing that we had landed on less than four months earlier. The German pilots were still not allowed to fly into Hong Kong, so we had an uneventful flight to Canton, where we were dumped on the tarmac at the end of the runway. We were told to wait for a plane that would take us on to Hong Kong. It was very hot, but after an hour or so the plane did arrive, and we finally made it to Hong Kong. In those days, anyone could go from southern China to Hong Kong without visas or permission of any kind. Because of this, refugees had been pouring into Hong Kong for months. Refugees of many different nationalities were to be found there, and accommodation of any kind was almost impossible to find. The Hong Kong government had put up nisan huts all along the northern shores of Kowloon, trying to accommodate the thousands who were arriving.

The morning we were to leave Chongqing, we received a cable from the only family we knew in Hong Kong saying, "Do not come, there is no accommodation available." But we had no alternative. Our flight was arranged with the St. Paul, and we had nowhere to stay in Chongqing anyway. The Canadian couple, who worked at the Hong Kong YMCA, had been on the boat with us from Vancouver to Shanghai. Donald had written to them asking if they could arrange some sort of temporary accommodation for us. We boarded the plane in Chongqing. We knew we had no accommodation waiting for us, but we simply said, "Lord, we trust You."

CHAPTER 6

VIA HONG KONG TO TAIWAN
Mid-May to June 11,1949

"He shall direct thy paths."
Proverbs 3:6

The hop from Canton to Hong Kong was quick, and by mid-afternoon we found ourselves at the Hong Kong airport. No one was there to meet us, because they had cabled us not to come.

"Lord, what should we do next?" we asked.

Soon we heard an announcement that the airport transport had a bus leaving for the Kowloon YMCA. Since that was where our friends worked, we boarded the bus and soon found ourselves at the Y. We had only just gotten our luggage inside the door when we heard our names being called. There were our friends, all smiles, delighted to see us.

"While you were in the air," they told us, "accommodation has been found for you at the Bishop's house. We are so glad you decided to come despite our cable." Once again we saw the Lord's wonderful provision for our family. He goes before and prepares the way, what have we to fear? "I sought the Lord, and He answered me; He delivered me from all my fears" (Psalm 34:4).

They soon took us over to Hong Kong Island. The Bishop's house was situated half way up the Peak. In those days you had to take the car over on a ferry. That was all a part of the adventure, and Andrew was old enough to enjoy it, even though he was still running a low-grade fever.

Talk about the Lord's over and abundant provision. It was far more than we could have ever dreamed. A comfortable room, beds with clean sheets, a cot for Robin and even a good British meal was provided for the over fifty missionaries who were staying there at that time. Proverbs 3:5-6 constantly came to our minds: "Trust in the Lord with all your heart . . . He shall direct your paths." Each day Donald and I were learning more and more the wonder of implicitly following the directions in God's Word. We were experiencing the joy there is in following Jesus and not leaning to our own understanding, a lesson that would stand us in good stead throughout our lives.

A very interesting thing happened during our first meal there in the Bishop's home. A lady who was sitting next to Donald had just arrived back from Taiwan. When she heard that Donald was a medical doctor she said without any hesitation, "You are urgently needed in Taiwan." Donald's response was that he was a British trained doctor, and he and his family had been travelling almost nonstop for over seven months. He planned to get a job in Hong Kong as quickly as possible and settle down for a while. We had to learn once again during the next few days that the Lord's thoughts are not our thoughts, and His ways not our ways.

The next morning, we bundled the boys into a taxi and went to Queen Mary's Hospital where the doctors were already expecting us. Andrew and Robin were both immediately admitted, and extensive tests began. They lived in luxury for almost one week being thoroughly spoiled by doctors and nurses, and, because they were together, they did not seem to mind when we left them, which was a real blessing.

Meanwhile, when we got back to the Bishop's house, we had two more requests to go to Taiwan. The lady who had spoken to Donald the night before had apparently cabled her friends with the Canadian Presbyterian Mission in Taipei telling them she had found them a doctor! Their cable to us said, "Come over at our expense, and talk to us about it."

The second message was from the American Embassy. The airport officials had reported to them that a British doctor had arrived in Hong Kong from China. We learned later that both British and American authorities had been asked by the foreign community in Taipei to try to find a doctor coming out of China who would be willing to go to Taiwan. The only foreign doctor on the whole island was leaving the next week, and they were desperate for medical help for the foreign community.

With this third request in less than twenty-four hours, we began to sense we had better start praying about it. But still we really hoped for a job for Donald in the nice, safe British colony of Hong Kong. We had no desire to head off again into the great unknown. That afternoon, Donald went to the Hong Kong Medical Association and asked about getting a job in Hong Kong. The answer was, "We have plenty of doctors in Hong Kong. There are no vacancies at present, but there is an urgent need in Taiwan. Would you be willing to go to Taipei?"

The Lord was beginning to get the message through into our rather stubborn minds that His plan for us was to move on to Taiwan. We hardly knew where the island was. All we knew was that Donald's parents had served there for a while in 1927-28, when the English Presbyterian Mission pulled them out of China and sent them to work with the Canadian Presbyterians in Taiwan.

After sleeping on all these requests over our second night in Hong Kong, it seemed right for Donald to accept the offer to go over to Taipei and talk to the Canadian Mission leaders to find out more about the situation. I would stay in Hong Kong with the boys, who were still in Queen Mary's Hospital.

Donald flew over to Taiwan and was met by the Rev. James Dickson, Chairman of the Mission. He was given a great welcome, not only because he was desperately needed as a doctor, but also because there were some missionaries who remembered his parents working there. They even produced photographs of Donald as a small boy! This made him feel much more at home and seemed to confirm that we should go and work with them.

Donald was offered two separate possibilities. The first was to have the British or American Chambers of Commerce, along with other foreign companies, set up a medical office for him downtown where he would work directly with them. This would be strictly a business arrangement. The second was to have the Canadian Mission give him a room in Mackay Memorial Hospital where he could see the foreign patients, and we would become associates of the Mission on a year's contract, paid by the Mission. In this case, Donald would work full time at Mackay Hospital as the Medical Director and only have certain hours when he would see patients from the foreign community. We chose the latter; for, though we never called ourselves missionaries, we did not have any desire to be in the business world. We were out there strictly for the Lord and His work, whether medical or more directly "spiritual." We were there to live for Him. So we chose to go to Taiwan and work in the Canadian Presbyterian Mission Hospital following Donald's father's footsteps from twenty-two years earlier.

Meanwhile, back in Hong Kong, the boys were released from Queen Mary's and given a completely clean bill of health. Within twenty-four hours of arriving in Hong Kong their fevers were gone. Nothing was ever found, and the hospital doctors told us they had had other foreign children who lived in Sichuan who had run continual fevers, yet no cause could be found. The medical world was now calling it "Sichuan fever."

During the next few weeks, Donald was able to get registered as a licensed doctor in Hong Kong. This proved to be an important step as very few drugs and other supplies were available in

Taiwan in those days. Later, on a number of occasions, one of us flew on the American Embassy plane to Hong Kong to buy supplies for the hospital. We also would end up with a long grocery list for our friends as well as ourselves. Talk about killing two birds with one stone!

During our time in Hong Kong we went up the Peak in a cable car called the Peak Tram. We then walked the whole way round the peak, pushing Andrew and Robin in their pushchair. The views of Hong Kong harbor were fabulous! We could see ships from many nations sailing in and out of what today is one of the busiest harbors in the world.

We got to know some of the Brethren missionaries who had come out of China and also Dr. Donald Nicholls, an Australian doctor who was with them. He had recently arrived planning to go into China, but he was unable to because of the political situation. Both Shanghai and Nanjing had fallen to the Communists by early June.

One Sunday morning we were visiting at the Brethren Assembly. During the Breaking of Bread, Donald prayed out loud. At the end of the service, we were just chatting with different people when a lady said to Donald, "You must be from Honor Oak."

"How in the world did you know?" asked Donald.

"Because of the way you prayed," was her reply. We were stunned! Then amused. Later, we decided that we should consider what in our vocabulary needed to be dropped. We loved our brothers and sisters at H.O., but in the Far East we wanted to be known as Christians rather than a couple from a certain group of the Lord's children in London, England.

We did have one invitation to stay in Hong Kong from a Dr. and Mrs. Clift, who had been running a Christian clinic in the Colony for some years. Dr. Clift was ill and unable to carry on the medical work. However, Taiwan definitely seemed to be where the Lord was leading us. So, on June 11th 1949, along with eight Brethren missionaries, five small children and all our worldly possessions, we once again boarded the St. Paul and flew off into the unknown.

CHAPTER 7

EARLY YEARS IN TAIWAN
June 1949 to May 1955

"As for God, His way is perfect."
Psalm 18:30

Several hours later, we landed on a runway outside the city of Taipei. The Taipei Airport was almost as primitive as the one in Chongqing, a grass strip, but this time it sat in the middle of a field, not the middle of a river!

It was pouring rain, reminiscent of England on a summer's day, only it was much hotter and very humid. We saw a couple waiting near the only airport building. Dr. and Mrs. James Dickson, the leaders of the Canadian Presbyterian Mission, were waiting for us. The other passengers were met by one of the Brethren missionaries already on the Island, so our paths separated for the day. We were taken to the mission compound, where there were four large houses surrounded by grass and a good number of trees, right next door to the Mackay Memorial Hospital. We were to share one of the mission houses with an older couple who worked at the China Sunday School Association. We had the larger half of a two-story house that had been divided into two homes. We only shared the front entrance. Wide balconies ran the full length of the front of the building, and the upstairs balcony was completely screened in to keep the mosquitoes at bay. Despite this, we still needed to use mosquito nets at night.

When we went to the hospital, we were given a tremendous welcome. We were employed as associate missionaries. Our salary was small, but the comfortable housing was free. Our original contract with the Presbyterians was for one year, but we ended up living and working there for two years.

Soon after we arrived in Taiwan, Andrew became very ill with scarlet fever and pneumonia. We were so thankful when he made a quick and full recovery. Not long after that, I started experiencing severe morning sickness, and we realized another little one was on the way. Fortunately, we had two very sweet Taiwanese girls, sisters, who helped us in the home. They did all the shopping, housecleaning, laundry and so on. We also had a high school girl who spoke some English and who sometimes came just to watch the boys playing out in the compound. Since there was an understanding that the compound gates were never shut, someone had to be watching the children every moment they were outside. Only once did we lose Robin. He was found, quite unperturbed, many blocks away by a friend who recognized him and brought him home.

Tony was born on May 29th, 1950, in Mackay Hospital. I was in the foreign patient's ward. As soon as the doctor and nurse left for lunch, my pains increased, and Donald, who had fortunately stayed with me, found himself delivering our third son. This was not what he had planned to do, but I was fainting with every pain! So, with no time to scrub up, he frantically rushed to deliver our son. We called him Nigel Anthony, but because his older brothers could not say his name correctly, we started calling him Tony. The nickname stuck.

The medical situation left a lot to be desired. In 1940, when all the missionaries had to leave because of the war, the hospital was handed over to the care of the Formosan Church (Taiwan was still known as Formosa from its days as a Portuguese colony). The hospital had not had a full-time, foreign medical director since 1940 and was in a sorry state when we arrived. One of the first things Donald had to do was set up a laboratory. No tests of even the simplest kind were being attempted. The end of a corridor was partitioned off, and a small and simple laboratory was opened. Fortunately, Donald had brought his medical books out of China. He was able to teach himself how to run a laboratory, and he later taught another doctor all the procedures.

As there were no other foreign doctors on the Island at this time, Donald had to care for Taipei's entire foreign population of about five hundred. Missionaries from central and southern Taiwan had to come 250-300 miles and more to see a western doctor. If anyone was too ill to travel, Donald had to make a house visit. Within the first three months of our being there, he had to travel south several times, and two missionaries who were seriously ill had to be sent to their respective homelands. The Lord wonderfully helped Donald and gave him wisdom far beyond his own ability or medical experience.

Early in September, he had to go to Hong Kong to buy medical supplies for the hospital, as even basic things could not be bought in Taiwan. The American Embassy flew their plane to Hong Kong quite frequently and were always willing to take either Donald or me to purchase medical supplies for the hospital.

By the end of September 1949, Dr. Kristoffer Fotland of the Norwegian Alliance Mission arrived in Taiwan with his wife. They lived in another of the houses close to Mackay Hospital. Dr. Fotland was a surgeon who had just recently had to leave north China. He already spoke Mandarin Chinese, so he was a great help as a translator and as a surgeon. Once again the Lord had supplied beyond what we had asked or thought. Over the next year or two, several other missionary doctors and nurses arrived in Taiwan, and the Mennonite Mission started a hospital in Hualien on the east coast, so the pressures on Donald became less and, we had more freedom to get involved with other things as the Lord directed.

By July 1951, some major disagreements had arisen between the Mission and the Taiwanese Presbyterian Church leaders who were still officially responsible for the hospital after the war. Unfortunately, this resulted in all the western staff being asked, by the Presbyterian Mission, to leave. The other missions reassigned their folk to different medical facilities. We were the only ones who did not belong to any mission organization. The Lord wanted us to stay in Taiwan. We were asked to set up in private practice for the sake of the foreign community. We moved to a small, rented Japanese house less than a mile from the hospital. This was the beginning of the Christian clinic that later became well known all over the Island for its medical work and other Christian outreaches such as the Triple C Camps. So, at the end of August, we moved into the rented house and set up the front room as a medical office. Donald was contracted to supply general practitioner services to various British firms who were pleading with us to stay in Taipei.

Rents at that time were very high. People were seeking to leave the island because of the uncertain political situation, and they wanted their money back fast. Those who were able to buy property could do so very cheaply. When our foreign friends found out that we were thinking we might have to leave because we were unable to pay the high rents, the British Chamber of Commerce and some British firms offered to help us buy a house if we would commit to staying in Taiwan. They paid the full amount up front, and the arrangement was that the contract money from each firm would go towards paying off the debt month by month. The remainder was a loan, free of interest for eighteen months. After that, we would need to start paying interest.

We saved hard, were as frugal as we could possibly be, and by the eighteenth month were able to pay off the loan in full. This, in itself, was a miracle of the Lord's wonderful provision to set Donald up in general practice. Exactly three years to the month after we had flown into Taiwan, we were in our own home. It was to be our home for the next twenty-seven years. Our three boys all called this "home," and, although they had a few years in England at a British boarding school, they all ended up in high school in Taiwan and graduated from American schools there.

When we flew into Taiwan on June 11th, 1949, we never dreamed we would be there for just over thirty years. The Lord's thoughts are truly not our thoughts, nor His ways our ways, but His ways are always the best.

During our two years working with the Presbyterian Mission, we were both studying Mandarin Chinese with dear Brother Huang from the church we were attending. He spoke almost no English, and, although at first this seemed difficult, in the end it was to our advantage. We were forced to use what little Chinese we knew. We soon discovered that we could often use the Bible almost like a dictionary, so we learned the names of the books of the Bible in Chinese. Then, understanding the words for chapter, verse, and the numbers, we could locate the verse he was seeking to use, and often figure out the meaning of a word. This helped our Bible study as well as our language study. We found out, too, that Brother Huang had a remarkable knowledge of the Bible. The myth that we, as missionaries, had come to teach the Chinese about the Lord and His Word was soon dispelled. Many of the Chinese Christians had a far greater knowledge of the Bible than we did, even though we had a pretty good grounding in the Word from our background at Honor Oak. We discovered that we had wonderful teachers of the Word around us, and precious brothers and sisters in the Lord. We thanked God for them, and we had tremendous fellowship with them. The Lord had quickly linked us up with a local church. Witness Li, a co-worker of Watchman Nee, was leading the church. Because of the connection that Honor Oak had with Watchman Nee, we did not look further for our church home in Taipei. It was quite a long bike ride to get to the meetings, but everyone rode bikes in those days, and we were used to that anyway.

During these early years in Taiwan, Donald had many opportunities to teach Bible classes in English, which gave us personal contacts with those hungry to know more about the Lord. We also helped to start a Sunday afternoon English service at the YMCA downtown, so that those who did not speak Chinese could have one service a week in English. Missionaries were beginning to arrive by the end of 1950. By 1951, a lot of missionaries to China were being allowed by their mission boards to come to Taiwan. Before 1950, very few missions allowed their people to travel straight from China mainland to Taiwan, like we had done. They felt that the political situation was too uncertain, and the likelihood of the Communists following the Nationalists to Taiwan was considered very high in those days.

So it was that less than one year after we left the Presbyterian Mission compound, we found ourselves in our own home, with the medical clinic under the same roof. Donald's office quickly became known as "Doctor Dale's Clinic." But, we knew that another doctor would soon be needed, so we changed the name to "Christian Clinic." It was not long before the clinic was also home, hospital, and hotel. It was "home" for our family, "hospital" for clinic patients who could not afford to pay the hospital fees, and "hotel" to the missionaries who came from other parts of the Island and needed somewhere to stay while in Taipei. Hotels were expensive and scarce. Mission headquarters had not begun to appear at that time, and most missionaries had very small homes, not at all conducive to having overnight guests. Our new building had plenty of floor space with the Japanese tatami. Tatami mats, typical floor covering in all Japanese houses, are made out of dried grass and are six by three feet in size.

We enjoyed our visitors and got to know many missionaries. I am still in touch with many of the people who stayed with us. On one occasion, a family of six came to stay with us. They also brought a friend with them. I am still in touch with the family, and in a recent email I discovered that their oldest son is actually a fifth generation missionary to China. Praise the Lord for families like this. Today, almost fifty years later, I have an address list filled with the names of people like these, who still receive my rather infrequent newsletters. "Friends are friends forever, if the

Lord's the lord of them." This is part of the chorus of a lovely song I recently learned, sung by George Beverly Shea. Friends are very precious, and I thank the Lord I have many of them.

At this time in Taiwan, students in the schools and universities were under much pressure not to get involved in Christian activities. Bible classes in military or government establishments were also being closed down. Students were getting expelled for refusing to bow down to the picture of Sun Yat Sen, the founder of the Chinese Republic. It was a requirement at any school function in those days. This, in turn, caused problems in the church, as some felt there was no religious significance while others felt it was very important in the light of Exodus 20:4-5, "Thou shalt not bow down to any image of anything in heaven or earth." The missionary community actually got together for a day of prayer, seeking the Lord concerning this. Later on, the government did loosen up a bit because of pressure brought on them by the Generalissimo and Madam Chiang Kai Shek. This was a reminder of the power of prayer in any given situation: "For we wrestle not against flesh and blood but against principalities and powers, and the rulers of the darkness of this age" (Ephesians 6:12).

Prayer became more and more important to us. The weekly prayer meeting in our home became a central focus point from which we moved only after clear direction from the Lord. This meeting also drew together Christians from the different embassies, the business world, and various missionary societies. We began to experience in a very real way that we were truly all one in Christ Jesus. We all shared the desire to be shining lights for Him in the midst of the darkness.

Certain things were prayed over more and more frequently during those early prayer meetings, and the need for a Bible school was one of the most urgent. It was not long before the first one opened, and we rejoiced at the answer to prayer. (At a considerably later date, that same prayer group started saying, "No more, Lord! Please no more!") Another prayer that was answered quite quickly was the need for more medical doctors. By May of 1952, there were five foreign doctors, including Donald, on the Island, and some of them had previously been in mainland China and already spoke Mandarin.

During our first few years in Taiwan, several quite important things were started. More and more westerners were arriving, and there was an immediate need for an English-speaking school. Since most of those arriving were Americans, it became apparent that the curriculum should be American. So, our British doctor helped Mrs. Andrew Loo, of the Pocket Testament League, and several other missionaries to start an American school. Some important lessons were learned in the ensuing months. They made a big mistake in relation to the board of directors. Of course, when the school was started by a group of missionaries, they were planning for a "Christian school." A fine principal was found in Miss Edna Merritt, from the U.S. Donald and I had met Miss Merritt on our travels to China in

1948. She was available and happy to come to Taipei, having previously worked in China some years before. Taipei American School was started with a Parents Board officially behind the school.

This worked extremely well for the first year or two, but, as the American military began to arrive in considerable numbers, the situation changed. They were known as the Military Assistance Advisory Group (M.A.A.G.), and it was not long before the Parents Board had changed from being all missionaries to being dominated by business, embassy, and military families who were not interested in the Christian aspect of the school. What the Christians had started was lost to secular education.

An important lesson had been learned. When Morrison Academy started in 1952, four mission boards took full responsibility. The school was founded on the clear understanding that those mission boards were responsible for the school. In fact, Miss Edna Merritt was also the first principal of Morrison Academy when it became clear she was going to have to resign from Taipei American School. So, although it was sad to see what T.A.S. became in the years to follow, it was good to have learned an important lesson early on.

We soon began to understand more fully just how important it was for us to be "tentmakers," and not to be with a missionary society. A western couple that worked with the railway applied to have their names included in the Taiwan Missionary Directory and were turned down because "they were not missionaries." When we heard this, Donald made it known that we would resign, because we were not with a missionary society either. By this time, we were fully accepted as missionaries (even if we did not call ourselves such), but our stand caused those responsible for this decision to think again. Eventually, the couple was told that their request had been reconsidered, and their names would be included in the directory after all.

Around this time, the "Saturday Morning Bible Club" was started. Some called it the Children's Bible Hour. It was really Sunday school on Saturday for the English-speaking children. It began in the spring of 1951, in downtown Taipei at the YMCA. To begin with, I was teaching the teenagers. It soon became apparent that the mothers who brought their children to the Y were getting rather tired of hanging around for an hour or more waiting for their children. By the fall of 1952, we offered to start an adult class for them, and the proposal was enthusiastically received. It was a wide open door, and I was the one chosen to teach the class. In the next few years, we had the joy of seeing a number of these mothers come to know the Lord.

When this began to happen, we soon had requests from the wives for something for their husbands. The result was what we called " the Couples Club," and one evening a week we got together as couples to study God's Word. We had some great times together. The couples were from business, embassy, military and missionary families. Some already knew the Lord and wanted the Bible study and fellowship, while others were seeking to find out why their friends were getting so excited about knowing the Lord Jesus.

Years later, we received a wonderful letter from an American couple who had attended that class quite regularly but returned to the States still not knowing the Lord. They wrote to tell us they had both been truly born again and were forever thankful for what they had learned in Taiwan, even though it was some years later that they really gave their lives to Jesus. What a joy to know that the seeds planted in the mid-fifties were still growing in the seventies and bearing much fruit. I am reminded of what the Apostle Paul wrote to the Corinthians: "Who then is Paul, and who is Apollos, but ministers through whom you believed, as the Lord gave to each one? I planted, Apollos watered, but God gave the increase" (I Corinthians 3:5-6). We thank the Lord that He gave us the privilege of planting the seeds, and, later, He let us know of the fruit in the lives of this couple.

The last part of a letter we wrote in May 1952 has a good summary of these early years. This was written the month before we moved to our permanent location, which became known island-wide as the Christian Clinic:

> Spiritually, the hearts of the mainland refugees (about 3 million) are still wide open to the Gospel, although there are signs that barriers are being raised in certain quarters, despite the whole-hearted support of the Generalissimo and his wife for the Christian activities. Please pray that the doors may be kept open.

Amongst the local Taiwanese population there is a much slower response, but, with the increased number of missionaries (now about 130), it is hoped that very soon every person on the Island may have had an opportunity to hear the Gospel. Bible Schools are appearing in different parts of the Island, and two more will soon be started. Missionary doctors now number five. The prayer meeting held weekly in our home usually numbers around twenty Taipei missionaries. Usually this number is doubled every month. These times of prayer cannot be too highly valued, since they bring together missionaries of many groups in their common desire for the blessing of the Lord upon this needy island.

As a family, we are all keeping in good health, for which we do thank the Lord, and Donald is only troubled by his asthma on occasion. The children, except for all having had measles, have been very well indeed.

Our "hotel" turned out to be not only for the overnight guests, but also for a few "long termers." One of these was Kari Torjesen who later became Mrs. Bob Malcolm, the author of "Women at the Crossroads" and a number of other books. Kari's brother, Ed, was working in southern Taiwan and asked us if we could give his sister a bed for three or four nights while she found out where the National Taiwan University planned for her to live. They had promised her accommodation as an English teacher. Of course we said, "Yes." The university accommodation never materialized, and Kari lived with us for well over a year before moving to live at Campus Crossroads, immediately opposite the university main gates. "All things work together for good." So many good things came about because of this. It really could be said that it became a life-changing experience, not just for Donald and I, but for many others. Kari had been closely associated with the Navigators while at the University of Minnesota. When she started to teach at Tai Da (the National Taiwan University in Taipei) in the fall of 1952, she soon found opportunities to share about the Lord. She would come back to our home and share with us over the supper table how this girl and that girl had found the Lord. Not too many weeks went by before those girls were leading their friends to accept Jesus as their Savior. It was exciting, but it was also quite baffling to me. I had been out on the so-called "mission field" for more than three years and had never led anyone to the Lord. Why? What was different about Kari?

One night, when Donald was out teaching a Bible class, and the three boys were already in bed and asleep, I picked up courage and knocked on Kari's door. "Come in," she called, and I opened the door. "Kari," I said, "how come you have led so many girls to the Lord so quickly, and I have been here more than three years and never led anyone to the Lord?"

"Come on in," she said. "Let's have a chat."

I shall never forget that evening! I can see us now, sitting in that little bedroom in Christian Clinic, while Kari asked me to share with her how I became a Christian. I quickly realized that she was making sure that I was really a Christian myself before she was going to share with me her secret in leading others to the Lord! That was quite humiliating. She had lived in my home for some weeks by this time; did she really not know that I knew the Lord? I guess she finally was satisfied that I did, and then we went on to talk about leading others to the Lord. She pointed me to II Timothy 2:2: "The things that you have heard from me among many witnesses, commit these to faithful men who will be able to teach others also." This was my introduction to what the Navigators called "the two-two program." Kari began to meet with me weekly and teach me from the Word how to lead others to the Lord. It was an exciting time and a time of real growth in practical application of the Word to my life, and to the lives of others.

By the following summer, 1953, many young men and women at the university had come to know the Lord. Follow-up became an important issue, and both my husband Donald, and Doug Sparks, the official leader of the Navigator ministry in Taiwan, had a part in this side of the work. Doug also taught classes for the students and, by that time, for more and more missionaries who were getting involved with the 2:2 program. Since these classes needed to be in the evenings, for the sake of the students, it became apparent that a daytime class was needed for the missionaries and other westerners who were keen to get in on what the Lord was doing. I was asked to teach this new class and had the joy of passing on the things I was learning, which indelibly printed on my own mind many more precious truths from the Word of God.

Kari, meanwhile, was enjoying growth in numbers and spiritual maturity amongst her girls at the university, and she had more and more opportunities for counseling outside of her classes. After a couple of months of teaching, she found the office that the university provided was inadequate for spiritual talks with the students, and so she rented a consultation room near the campus. Souls were saved, and as the family of God grew, a class was started to feed the newborn babes. Soon, they were sitting on the floor with straight backs and knees up, each girl afraid of hogging too much space. Another room and a hallway were rented in the same house. One day, Kari took all the Japanese doors down to survey the area and discovered, to her great delight, that there was a perfect meeting hall. Next, the Lord provided an organ and chairs, and the Sunday Gospel Hour was started. Weekdays saw the little place divided into a reading room and consultation room with students in and out for chats geared to bring the claims of Christ before them. So began what later became known as "Campus Crossroads."

"Who has despised the day of small things?" (Zech.4:10-a)

These very small beginnings soon began to grow. Kari expressed it well in a letter she wrote in the summer of 1954:

>On New Year's Eve, Roy Robertson, Oriental Navigators Director, challenged us to ask great things of a

Great God for 1954. I thought of my tiny, little, back-yard apartment and daringly asked for a HOUSE. God answered in January. Dr. Bob Pierce walked into Campus Crossroads one day and reviewed the area in which we squashed seventy students together. The Lord worked in his heart, we prayed together, and he left Taiwan with the promise that he would present the needs of Campus Crossroads to the Christian public in the States. "The Lord has done great things for us, whereof we are glad" (Psalms 126:3).

No one was allowed to hold Christian meetings on the university campus, so it quickly became clear that the non-Christian students were not being reached. Christian students went to their respective churches on Sunday mornings, but few non-Christians were going with them. The Lord gave us a new strategy. Invitations were prepared inviting students to Campus Crossroads on Sunday afternoons. With the invitation was a copy of the tract, "The Reason Why," by Robert Laidlaw. The Christian students helped Kari distribute them each week. They prayed that, before the end of the year, every student on campus would have received an invitation to the meeting. Those who did not respond to the invitation would at least have had an opportunity to clearly understand the Gospel message.

One day, a letter from the States asked Kari, "Was there a Campus Crossroads in Taiwan before you went there?"

"No, there wasn't," she answered, "but the idea did not start in my mind. My part has merely been to move step by step, according to His leading. We started small, but this is where the Lord has led us, and we rejoice that His Word is a 'lamp to our feet and a light to our path'" (Psalm 119:105). How wonderful to know that He directs our path as we acknowledge Him in everything (Proverbs 3:6)! Kari had the joy of living in the new, three-story Campus Crossroads for a couple of months with seven girls before it was time for her to return to the States to get married. One of these girls, Florence Chang, now Mrs. John Lin, had earlier been sent by the Lord to assist Kari in this challenging work. Florence had lived with Kari since the night, in August 1953, when she left the comforts of home and loved ones and stepped out into the darkness to follow Christ.

"My God shall supply all your needs according to His riches in glory by Christ Jesus" (Philippians 4:19). This wonderful promise covers every area of life . . . including finances. I have already mentioned that the British Chamber of Commerce, along with several British firms with whom Donald had contracts for medical services, had put up a loan, free of interest for eighteen months. By the eighteenth month, we were able to pay off this debt, so we paid no interest whatsoever and became the proud owners of our first home. Having completed the payment on the house, the next urgent need was a car. Every day Donald would cycle at least ten miles back and forth to Mackay Hospital to see any of his patients who needed hospitalization. He had visiting privileges, so he was able to continue to care for his own patients even when they had to be put in hospital. He was also doing many house calls, and, in those days, house calls often involved long distances by bicycle, with his heavy black bag carefully tied on the rack behind him. It was not unheard of for him to arrive back at the clinic looking forward to a meal with the family only to get an urgent call from the hospital. There were not any cell phones in those days to save him many hours riding back and forth.

A little over a year after the house was fully paid for, we were thrilled with the arrival of our first car. Rather than ease the pressures of work, this actually resulted in more work. The good part, however, was that Donald was not quite so exhausted as when he had to make the long bicycle rides each day, and the extra things accomplished were all important. We, and many others, were rejoicing in this provision from the Lord. How good He is!

Soon after we got our car, the first University Mission was held, October 12-18, 1953. Paul Shen, a beloved young Chinese pastor from Taichung, was our main speaker. The meetings were held on a small plot of land opposite the side entrance to the National Taiwan University, under three tents that had been bound together so that each supported the other. There was much prayer that there would be no typhoons during that week, or undoubtedly the tents would have been blown down. Every night saw increasing numbers of students coming out to the meetings, until, on the last evening, there was not enough room under the tents for the approximately seven hundred people present. During the course of the week, about fifty students and thirty others came to a decision to follow the Lord. Many of them attended the special followup classes that were then arranged. The Christian students who were involved in the 2:2 program were encouraged to personally try to help their friends.

Sometime later, the Presbyterian "Friendship Corner" and Grace Baptist Church and student center were built on this plot of land. Campus Crossroads was the forerunner, but more mission groups began to work with the students in one way or another. By the time Kari left, Campus Crossroads became known as Campus Evangelical Fellowship, an indigenous work led directly by the Chinese. Donald continued to be involved in an advisory capacity, along with David Adeney, of the British Inter Varsity Fellowship, who periodically came over from Hong Kong. Donald was often asked to speak at meetings in these and other student centers, and many students found the Lord in those years.

We often used to pray against Donald getting caught by a medical emergency when we planned an outing with the boys. He was always on duty, because we did not have a second doctor during our early years at Christian Clinic. We did manage trips to the beach at Tansui from time to time. Swimming was always popular. One memorable day, we went out into the country for a picnic. Donald had parked the car, and we were walking along the side of the road while the children were running in the fields beside us. Suddenly, Robin sank into the ground on which he was running and almost vanished out of sight! There was such a hard crust formed by the hot sun over the night soil pit that it looked no different than the rest of the ground, but with Robin's weight it immediately gave way. Villagers nearby quickly rescued him, and others rushed for water to wash him and his clothes, but poor Robin was desperately embarrassed by the whole affair. It really was very funny, but he felt so terrible about it that we tried hard not to laugh. Our picnic that day ended with Robin going home in Donald's vest (sleeveless pullover as we British would call it). We had our fun times and adventures as well as all the so-called "work"!

Andrew and Robin both started Chinese Nursery School before we moved to our permanent home on Hsin Sheng South Road. They enjoyed this very much and were, for more than a year, in the same kindergarten as two of the Generalissimo's grandchildren. Several times our children were invited to play at their home, which was not only close to the school they all attended, but also very close to our rented home. After Taipei American School opened, Andrew, and later on Robin, went there. Andrew was the only British child, so he represented England in a school photograph showing six or seven different nationalities, when the school first started. When Robin started 1st grade, class was only in the mornings, so he continued in the

Chinese School 1st grade in the afternoons. This kept him busy and out of mischief! Tony only attended Chinese Kindergarten up to the time we left for England in the spring of 1955. He first got his name in the local newspaper when he sang "Ba-Ba Black Sheep" and "Jesus Loves Me" on a radio program beamed into China mainland. Chinese was his first and only language until we were on the boat, and he had to make the effort to be understood by those around him. Most of that month on the boat, he continued to speak to both his brothers and Donald and me in Chinese, but as soon as we landed in UK that all changed.

I have jumped a bit ahead of our story, and I need to take you back to the miracles that happened in the final months in Taiwan, before we were able to set out on the long voyage back to UK—our first leave.

CHAPTER 8

OUR FIRST LEAVE
April 1955 to November 1956

"Trust in the Lord with all your heart, and lean not on your own understanding."
Proverbs 3:5

Excitement heightened as our seventh Christmas away from England approached, and arrangements were beginning to fall into place for us to take some leave. At least, that was what we thought! Dr. Donald Nicholls and his family were expected to arrive from Australia in March, and we had hoped to take a trip around Taiwan to update ourselves on the Island-wide situation before leaving at the end of April. As is so often the case, our plans turned out not to be the Lord's plans. We had to learn not just to have mental assent to James 4:13-15, but to believe it when the Bible says, "You do not know what will happen tomorrow . . . You ought to say, If the Lord wills, we shall live and do this or that." These were important lessons He wanted to teach us, and our prayer partners, before He considered us ready to go on leave.

When one walks with the Lord, life is often full of surprises. In our Christmas 1954 Newsletter, Donald wrote:

If anyone had suggested that, at the end of a six-year term in China, a great deal of our time would be taken up with evangelistic opportunities and Bible teaching amongst the American population here, I, for one, would not have believed it. But, incredible as it may seem, that is the way God has led. Penny is now responsible for the Mother's Class that runs in conjunction with the Children's Bible Hour. There are usually about fifteen to twenty people present and she is able to use several of the mothers from her Women's Training Class to teach for her, thus lightening her own load and providing excellent training for them. Most of them have only become Christians this past year and of course have never taught before. On the men's side the response has not been so great, but we are seeing the Lord bring many from half-heartedness into a real zeal for the Lord. Numbers are increasing slowly, and we are praying that the Lord will provide His chosen ones to carry on the work while we are away. Out of these two classes has arisen the Taipei Christian Couple's Club that meets Thursday evening for fellowship around the Lord's Word, and for coffee and cakes afterwards. In the middle of November we had a special effort with Dr. James Graham as guest speaker. More than forty came for the buffet supper and to hear Dr. Graham speak. Many were brought under conviction, and we are looking to the Lord to use Couple's Club for His glory in the days ahead.

Then came a challenge to prayer. Dr. Don Nicholls' wife, Margot, was expecting again, and since she was Rhesus negative they felt they must stay in Australia until after the baby was born. Could we delay until the fall?   It seemed impossible for us to consider delay because of the boys' schooling and their need to have some months in England with us, to improve their spoken English before entering boarding school. We seriously considered my going ahead with the boys as we already had bookings on the S.S. Chusan from Hong Kong to leave May 2nd. People in the Couple's Club and many others started praying very specifically. Five days before we were due to leave, an American doctor, Dr. John West, phoned from Los Angeles saying he had heard of our need from Kari Torjesen, and he and his wife could be ready to come by early June. Already another doctor in Taiwan had said if a replacement was on the way then he could arrange to stand in the gap for a few weeks, to enable Donald to travel with the family. What rejoicing there was when we realized that the Lord was making the impossible, possible, in His perfect timing! We all left together on April 25th, 1955 heading for Hong Kong, and, after several days there, we boarded the ship for the United Kingdom.

We had a wonderful trip; the sun was shining almost the whole way. In Singapore, Donald, Andrew and Robin set off up through the Malay Peninsula to see a little of what was being done for the Lord amongst the Chinese in the "New Villages." Donald had a cousin working in Malaysia, as well as other friends to meet along the way. They saw something of the immense problems that were faced by those engaged in what was then a relatively new kind of work. They better understood the strain of living constantly behind barbed wire, surrounded by sullen and suspicious people who regarded them as British agents rather than ministers of Christ. Hitchhiking on jeeps, trucks and any other form of transportation that came their way, they went from village to village and had many adventures. They almost failed to get back to the Chusan in Penang before we sailed. I have never been more grateful to see Donald and the two boys than I was an hour before we were due to pull away from the dock.

The rest of the journey was pretty uneventful. Tony had his 5th birthday the day before we landed at the London docks. The Captain gave a special birthday party in his honor. After forty-five years, I still have the birthday card given by Captain Bodley and the ship's company. On May 30, 1955, more than six and a half years after that rainy Sunday afternoon when we had sailed down the Clyde from Glasgow headed for China, we once again set foot on British soil. By nightfall we had arrived at the Vicarage, Great Chesterford, near Cambridge, where my mother lived and kept house for her brother, the vicar. This was to be our home and base of operations for the next sixteen months. The children loved the big garden. It had plenty of play space and areas to run around. There was also a small river at the foot of the garden where white swans would lazily swim back and forth. Everything was so new and wonderful to the boys; they ran from one new thing to another and back to us excitedly wanting to tell us the next thing they had seen. They were often unable to express their excitement, either in English or Chinese. This, at times, became quite frustrating to them, and it quickly confirmed to us how important it was to help them with the language. Everything seemed to be a new experience after the confines of the Christian Clinic yard. We were all so thankful for this lovely place we could call home while in England.

We had a happy summer visiting family and friends. The only mishap was when Robin broke his arm falling off a donkey in southern Ireland, while we were staying with Marta. This resulted in Donald having to go ahead to the Keswick Convention without us. He took Andrew with him. Robin, Tony and I followed some days later, just in time for the last days of the convention. We had the privilege of staying with the Officers Christian Union (O.C.U.) house party where we were much encouraged by meeting some who had been praying for us regularly for many years.

After Keswick, we were able to attend the August Bank Holiday weekend conference at Honor Oak, a real treat after our years away. We also visited Donald's parents in Scotland, and then helped at the Elie CSSM (Children's Special Service Mission). My mother was able to come to Elie with us and was a part of the team in the house, cooking and preparing meals. The children loved to join in building the sand pulpit each morning, decorating it with shells and wild flowers. They would often write a Bible verse across the front of the pulpit, usually the verse that was to be memorized that day.

While driving around England and Scotland we found ourselves spending a lot of time teaching the boys English. Such simple words as "hedge" or "fields" and names of animals and birds were all totally new to them. They hadn't seen any cows, sheep, sparrows or blackbirds in Taiwan, and we realized we should have been reading children's storybooks to them far more than we did. All in all, it was a full summer but a very enjoyable one. There were many opportunities to see family and friends, and also to help the boys adjust to the unfamiliar culture and to the English language.

During our time at the Elie CSSM, Donald had to fly to Denmark for a conference with Paul Madsen at Nyborg Strand. We were greatly privileged to have these opportunities for ministry in other countries, which not only increased our own world vision but also substantially increased the number of prayer partners we had. Later on, Paul accompanied T. Austin Sparks and his wife to Taiwan and other countries in the Far East ministering amongst the Chinese assemblies linked with Watchman Nee and known in the western world as the "Little Flock." In 1957 we had the joy of hosting them in Taipei, and I was able, along with Dr John West and a number of Chinese brothers and sisters, to travel around the Island with them visiting many of these assemblies.

After the CSSM, we returned as a family with my mother to Great Chesterford and began to prepare Andrew and Robin for boarding school, the same school Donald was left in at the age of six. They were excited about going and very proud of their new school uniform – gray shorts and shirts with pink ties, pink blazers, and gray knee socks with pink stripes. It was very different to anything they had ever worn in Taiwan. The day came to take them to Great Walstead, just south of London. They seemed excited to finally be going to boarding school. Donald and I were headed for the IVF mission in Southampton. That helped to soften the blow of parting with the two boys. Tony had already been left with my mother and was attending the "infant's school" in Great Chesterford. In Southampton, over two hundred students and graduates were combing the city for Christ, helping in outreach to new students and in the churches cooperating in the mission.

Throughout our time in the UK, we were very conscious of the Lord directing our paths. Once the boys were all in school, we were based at the guesthouse at Honor Oak, usually known as "The Center." We had the opportunity to spend time with many old friends, and to make new ones. It also enabled us to regularly get to the prayer meetings, Bible studies, and Sunday services (when not speaking ourselves elsewhere). During this time, we were also getting invitations for meetings in the U.S., in the spring. The Lord was confirming to us that He wanted us to go to America after the boys went back to school in January. We saw Him clearly directing our path and providing all that was needed. For example, Tony would be staying with my mother for some months, and, during the Easter vacation, Andrew and Robin would also be with her. My mother needed help if she was going to take on this added responsibility. A dear au pair from Switzerland, who was working at the Center, indicated to us that she would love to go and work for my mother during that period. Donald and I were hesitant to take her away from the Center, where we knew she would be greatly missed. However, Hildegaard went with us to discuss it with Mrs. Taylor, who was in charge of the guesthouse, and the final decision was that Hildegaard would move to help my Mum. She proved to be invaluable. She was very good with Tony, and it all worked out well.

Donald helped with the London University mission in early January, and then as soon as the boys returned to Great Walstead, we got on the boat to New York. We were in the States for four and a half months. Soon after we arrived, it became apparent that I was expecting. I struggled with morning sickness for some weeks, but we managed to keep to our schedule in spite of it. In Minneapolis, while we were staying with Bob and Kari Malcolm, I actually had to have some days in bed. We had many wonderful answers to prayer while with the Malcolms. The opportunity arose to drive a car for an agent from Minneapolis to Seattle, Washington; even the gas (petrol) was paid for, and the number of days we were allowed to use the car before delivering it were far more than we needed. It was a wonderful provision from the Lord, and the cheapest way to travel. Not only that, but we saw much more of the country by driving. The trip across the Rockies was particularly spectacular. We had brilliant sunshine, and quite a lot of the winter snow was still hanging around. We were constantly praising the Lord for the beauty of His creation as we drove almost four full days before we finally reached Seattle.

Having delivered the car, we drove on from Seattle down to Los Angeles. Dr. John West's sister, Lou, who lived in Seattle on a boat, loaned us her car, and once again the natural beauty and incredible contrasts of different parts of the States became apparent to us. We went through the Redwood National Park in northern California, where we saw ancient trees including some of the world's tallest. In Los Angeles, we stayed with friends from H.O. and had a number of meetings with them. The Lord was giving us more and more of a world vision and linking us up with those who would follow us in prayer in the years ahead.

While we were in Los Angeles we also had the joy of a day with Dr. John West. We had never met before, even though he was taking our place at Christian Clinic. He had had to fly a patient to England and was returning to Taiwan via the States. The Lord's ways truly are beyond anything we could ever ask or dream. We were so grateful to be able to talk and pray together that day, and discuss plans for the work at Christian Clinic once there were two doctors rather than just one.

We continued to pray for the Lord's provision for us to drive back east from Los Angeles, but friends were not hopeful and all told us that we were very unlikely to be able to find a car in that direction. Well, with the Lord all things are possible! Our friend from Taipei, Helen Gilkerson, had a friend in Columbus, Ohio, who had been left a car by someone who had recently died in Los Angeles. The folk in Ohio asked Helen if she, or any friend of hers, would be willing to drive the car across the country. There was no hurry. Whoever brought it could take as long as they needed to. When Helen told them about us, they were delighted to lend it to us. They even said we could drive all the way to the East Coast, use it as long as we needed to and then Donald could deliver it to them just before we left for England. When he finally did take it to them, they handed him a plane ticket to fly back to New York. The Lord had provided us with cars all along the way, from coast to coast. Hallelujah!

We spoke at many meetings with university students, young people's groups and in different churches. We had a wonderful weekend with the Navigators at their recently acquired head-quarters, at Glen Eyrie, in Colorado Springs. Sadly, in Louisville, Kentucky I had a miscarriage and was two days in hospital. Even with this disappointment, we knew the Lord was saying to us, "Trust Me with your whole heart; I know what is best for you and for your family." Our time in the States had given us renewed contact with many we had known in Taiwan, some who had been Donald's patients, some who were fellow-workers for the Lord, and many who had been in Couples Club or other Bible study groups. What a privilege to travel for Him!

We were back on board ship headed once again for the UK. We arrived in time for Andrew and Robin's half-term long weekend. The rest of the summer was spent in England. During the vacation, the whole family went to David Tryon's boy's camp in Anglesey, North Wales. It was all under canvas, and it rained a great deal of the time, but, despite that, it was much enjoyed. Donald had worked with David while he was still at Monkton (the boarding school Donald attended), so he was familiar with the camping program as well as the surrounding area. Sadly, these camps had had to close down during the war, but by 1956 they had already been going again for a number of years, and each year many boys were finding the Lord there. So, the summer passed, and Andrew and Robin had to return to Great Walstead, but not before the Lord had wonderfully led in the provision of surrogate parents. Dr. John Roche and his wife Myrtle offered to act as official guardians to the boys. They visited them at Great Walstead, took them out at half-terms and gave them a wonderful Christmas. They did all the things we, as parents, would love to have done.

A few weeks before we expected to leave England, the shipping company contacted us to say our ship would have to go via the Cape of Good Hope because of the closure of the Suez Canal. This was going to add two weeks to our journey and 20% to the cost of our tickets. We had the option to cancel or pay the increase. My brother Neil offered to pay the increase, and we were able to go ahead with the planned departure date. There were many other missionaries on board. We were travelling on a passenger liner this time, not a freighter. We had lots of good fellowship and regular times of Bible study and prayer. One family we got to know well was going to India. We continue to swap prayer letters after more than forty years. It was interesting to be able to get off the ship in Cape Town and take a cable car ride to the top of Table Mountain. Donald, Tony and I took a long walk up there. The air was invigorating, the views magnificent, and we wished we'd had time to stay there much longer. We returned to the ship, and a day or two later we found ourselves able to deboard again, this time in Durban. In Durban, a friend with the S.A.G.M. (South Africa General Mission) kindly picked us up and drove us inland to see some of the Zulu kraals. On the way back, there had been an accident on one of the smaller bridges which delayed us to the point where we wondered if we would find the ship had sailed without us. Fortunately this did not happen!

After stopping in Bombay, where most of the missionaries disembarked, we continued on to Hong Kong. After two days on a much smaller vessel across a very rough China Sea, we finally landed in Keelung, the northern port city of Taiwan, on November 12th, 1956. We had been away from Taipei for more than eighteen months. There, at the dockside, were John and Beverley West to welcome us and drive us back to Taipei. When we reached Christian Clinic, Kan, our faithful cook, was waiting at the door to greet us. We knew that we had arrived HOME.

CHAPTER 9

HOME AGAIN!   MINISTRY AND MEDICAL
November 1956 to 1960

"My God will meet all your needs."
Philippians 4:19

It was wonderful to be back home after so much travelling and great for Donald to have the help of Dr. West after having so many years in a single-handed practice. It was somewhat strange to have only Tony home and hard to think of Andrew and Robin so far away. News from them, however, told us they were enjoying life at Great Walstead.

One of the first surprises in the New Year (1957) was the six weeks visit of Mr. and Mrs. Austin Sparks from our home fellowship in London. Mr. and Mrs. Paul Madsen from Denmark came with them. They were all in Taiwan at the invitation of the Chinese Christian Assembly. Dr. John West and I had the privilege of travelling around the island with them and seeing just how extensive their work was in many parts of the island.

We were glad that the Sparks and Madsen's visit came at this time. We had been feeling it was important for Christian Clinic to be more closely linked with a local, indigenous Chinese church. As a result of these weeks together, we had a greatly increased sense of "belonging." Not long after their visit, one of the "home groups" began to meet at Christian Clinic, which was, of course, also our home. Brother and Sister Lin, along with Donald and I, were appointed as "Home Group Leaders," and we rejoiced in being able to be a closer part of this local fellowship.

In early July 1957, I took Tony back to England. By then he had finished second grade, and we were able to attend my brother Neil's wedding. As soon as school was over in England, I took the three boys to Ireland to stay with Marta, my guardian from childhood days. Andrew and Robin spent most of their time horseback riding, while Tony enjoyed the donkey, and we all enjoyed the countryside and the excursions we were able to take.

After Ireland, we went to a Christian Families Houseparty. To quote from my letter written before Christmas 1957, "This houseparty proved to be the perfect holiday when we were without 'Daddy,' as there were children of all ages and there was always something that each age group, boys or girls, would enjoy to do." We also had John and Myrtle Roche with us for part of this time. That was especially good for Tony, because he was able to get to know them a bit better before I was to leave him at Great Walstead at the end of the summer when they would become guardians for him.

While I was with the boys in England, Donald saw the Lord's provision in many different ways. He was able to help a young Chinese Christian worker who was taken seriously ill with asthma by inviting him to move into our home. This made it much easier for Donald to look after him. After this brother had recovered, he stayed on for a few weeks until the day of his wedding. Donald writes, "Fellowship with him throughout those weeks was a great blessing to me, and his presence a great help to the meetings taking place in our home at that time. Hardly had he moved out when a recently married couple moved in. The wife had been converted in our home several years before, just after leaving high school, and the husband, a young Chinese engineer, had found the Lord at the University Mission in which I assisted some five years ago." Donald enjoyed their company. He was grateful for the opportunity to get to know them better and was thankful not to be alone those months that I was away.

In the Chinese church the main item of interest was the decision to split up the existing six assemblies into twenty-eight smaller groups so there would be increased fellowship and a greater outreach in each local area. Meetings continued in our home as one of the twenty-eight small groups in Taipei at that time.

At Thanksgiving that year, Donald was asked to fill in for the U.S. Air Force Chaplain, who had the flu, by speaking at the Base Chapel for the special Thanksgiving service. This was an unexpected privilege. Donald had many opportunities to preach during this time, in both English speaking groups and Chinese. Aside from the speaking engagements, the medical work kept him extremely busy, especially when Dr. and Mrs. West had a sudden opportunity to go back to the States with their kids.

They were away for about six months and were truly missed by both office staff and patients.

Language study took most of my time once I got back from England in early November. I was preparing to enter the new missionary language school that had recently opened. For the next two years, this was my main occupation. My only break from language school was during the summer of 1958, when the three boys came home. During those seven weeks, Dr. West kindly took the full load of the medical work so Donald could devote all of his time to be with the children and me. The summer of 1958 also brought with it more violence. There was shooting every other day from the China mainland to the Islands of Quemoy and Matsu, which are only a few miles from the mainland but were still under the control of the Nationalists in Taiwan. Because of this, there was considerable tension on the political front that summer. Despite the shooting, we were able to go as a family south as far as Chia Yi and from there up the mountain to Alishan. It took seven hours on the train from Chia Yi to Alishan in those days. At the end of the summer, all three boys returned to Great Walstead. Tony only just made it, having had a rather severe upset tummy the last week of the vacation.

1959 was the only year that neither Donald nor I spent any time with the boys. However, it was also the year during which the decision was made for us to stay in Taiwan and for the boys to enter Morrison Academy. How we came to that decision comes in the next chapter. In the summer of 1960 they all three came home for the holidays. Andrew stayed and went into 9th grade at Morrison, while Robin and Tony went back to Great Walstead for one more year of school at the recommendation of the Morrison superintendent. The transition from the British system would be easier for Robin and Tony in 1961 when Robin could enter 9th grade and Tony 7th.

Once the decision was made for us to stay in Taiwan and for the boys to enter Morrison Academy, we were thinking long term. Taipei was home, and, as long as the boys were on the island, Donald and I would not both leave Taiwan together, even for a short period of time. The political situation was too unstable. China and Taiwan were still officially at war.

So, bringing the boys back to Taiwan in 1960 was actually instrumental in keeping us on the island for another twenty years. It was also the catalyst that saw Triple C Camps begin. That story comes next.

CHAPTER 10

HOW TRIPLE C CAMPS BEGAN
August 1960

**"My word . . . will accomplish what I desire, and achieve
the purpose for which I sent it."
Isaiah 55:11**

"Lord, Donald will never agree to bring the boys back to
Taiwan." I was thinking about his great desire to have them
go to Monkton Combe, the same boarding school where he had
studied. Tradition dies hard in the heart of a true British public
school boy.

"If You are really speaking to me, Lord, then please tell
Donald, too."

That was my reaction when I sensed the Lord in prayer one
morning, in December of 1959, telling me we should bring our
three boys back from England and put them into one of the
English-speaking schools in Taiwan.

My husband, Dr. Donald as his many patients often called
him, was up in the mountains of Central Taiwan on a combined
linguistic and medical team with Clare McGill. Clare was one of
the Canadian Presbyterian missionaries whose main work was to
put the different tribal languages in writing. Donald's main task,

however, was medical work. He usually spent most of his time pulling teeth on these trips, for there were no dentists available. If he was not extracting teeth, he was dispensing worm medicine to all the children because there was no way to do any lab tests, and the chances were that every child had worms anyway. While Donald took care of the medical side, Clare would teach the local tribal people how to read their own language.

Before they moved on to the next village, they would share the Gospel with those gathered. These trips were often very fruitful for the Kingdom—some came to know the Lord for the first time, others were hungry to know more of His life and His Word.

In the midst of this unlikely setting, the Lord spoke clearly to Donald about our children. When he returned home, during our first dinner back together again, he suddenly said to me, "You'll be surprised by this, but while I've been away, the Lord has been telling me that we should bring the boys back home. They can go to school in Taiwan."

"Hallelujah," I said. "The Lord has been saying the same thing to me. I told the Lord He would have to tell you Himself. I never could!"

"Well, it looks like the Lord answered your prayer," Donald said smiling.

That started our planning for our three sons to return to Taiwan. Little did we realize then how many lives would be affected by this decision, and how many young people would come to know the Lord because we made the choice to obey.

For us, the next step was to write and tell the boys of our decision and how excited we were at the thought of having them back on the Island. We waited expectantly for their response. In the English boarding school, students had to write a letter to their parents every Sunday afternoon before they could go outside to play, so we knew we would hear from them soon. Our younger two, Robin and Tony, made no comments.

Andrew, however, wrote, "It will be lovely to come back home, but there is one thing I shall miss very much: the boy's camp I have been to on the Easter vacation." We did not know until several years later when Andrew gave a testimony at Triple C, that he had made his first commitment to the Lord at this camp in England.

As we read Andrew's letter, I said, "Dick and Lucille Webster are building a camp site down in Tainan. Let's write to them and suggest we start a summer camp for the English-speaking young people in Taiwan."

"Yes, I was thinking the same thing," Donald said.

The Websters had a son who was very close in age to our Andrew and two other younger girls. We knew camps were very much on their hearts since they had bought this land and already begun to build the dining room and kitchen in preparation for starting Chinese University student camps and retreats. They were the ideal couple with whom to share this wonderful idea.

Within two or three days we had a letter back from the Websters, and the four of us had started to plan a summer camp for young people enrolled in the American schools. We had to limit it in this way, because we knew that otherwise we would be swamped with Chinese students wanting to learn English, and that, of course, was not the purpose of this particular project.

How often one step of obedience begins a line of events that the Lord has seen all along.

That first camp was planned for just one week in August 1960. Little did we realize when we said, "Yes," to the Lord and took that step of obedience to bring the boys back to Taiwan that it was going to affect the lives of so many young people in the ensuing years.

All missionary societies, English-speaking businesses, embassies, and other groups from the western world who were in Taiwan at that time were notified of the plans for the camp. Thirty-five young people were registered, but, when the great day actually arrived, fifty-five turned up at the Mount of Olives campsite. Both military and missionary kids poured in, and somehow we managed to fit them all into the little dormitory space that there was at that time. The Tainan U.S. Air Force Base personnel were extremely helpful and often brought in whole meals from the base to supplement what we could prepare in the camp kitchen. The Lord constantly brought to our attention how important it was that we should step out in faith to do his bidding, and how, then, He would supply our every need.

As that first camp was drawing to a close, the frequent question was, "When are we going to do this again?"

All the counselors were bombarded with comments such as, "We cannot wait for the next camp." "When can we have another one?" "Don't let's wait until next summer. That is too long!"

One of the campers asked, "What about a weekend retreat in the fall?"

This suggestion met immediately with a resounding "Yes," and it was decided that we would try to find a suitable place in the center of Taiwan for a weekend retreat.

Already the camp was being called "Dr. Dale's Camp," and Donald did not really want that. So, Sunday afternoon at the first retreat we had an open competition. All the campers were asked to go and pray that the Lord would give them ideas for a name for these retreats and camps. These suggestions were to be written down, handed in by a certain time, and then at the evening counselor's meeting they would be considered.

At the counselor's meeting that Sunday evening, we looked at these suggestions. One immediately stood out to us all and was unanimously chosen.

TRIPLE C CAMPS   (Christ Can Conquer became our motto)

So, the name for the camps was settled and quickly caught on all over the Island.

Then the Lord allowed us to face other challenging situations. I will share just one as an illustration. During our 1961 summer camp, we were again at the Mount of Olives in Tainan. At one of the evening meetings, the song leader suggested that we should all raise our hands in praise to the Lord as we were singing, "I will lift up my hands to the Lord." After the meeting, several counselors came to Donald, who was the camp director, and said that they strongly opposed such "Pentecostalism." Donald called a counselor's meeting after the young people were all in bed. We prayed together for some time. Then he said that he could not forbid anything that was so clearly in Scripture (Psalms 63:4, 119:48, 141:2; I Timothy 2:8, and other verses). He continued to explain that he had never before experienced the raising of hands in worship. However, he sensed the Holy Spirit had really been leading our song leader. Donald was on the platform at the time, and he had opened his eyes to see the response from the young people. He realized at once that they were truly worshipping the Lord. The matter was settled. If it was in Scripture, we should allow it. An important principle had been recognized and established for the future of the camps, as well as for our personal work and walk with the Lord. In later years, a number of those counselors and others who worked with us expressed an appreciation of Donald's leadership and his fearless determination to believe and act upon the Word, regardless of what others might say or think.

So, the decision to bring our three boys from school in England back to Taiwan was to be one of those "all things working together for good for those who love the Lord." You may be wondering why some parents found it so hard to bring their children away from their homelands and put them into an American school. One of the many reasons why missionaries from Europe often did not want to put their children into the American schooling system was because it usually ended up that the children then wanted to go to the States for university rather than back to their homeland. The next thing was an American boyfriend, (or girlfriend), a wedding and, before long, Mum and Dad were told their offspring would be applying for American citizenship. This did not appeal to most of the parents from Europe at that time!

How did the Lord show us personally what to do? Once again it was by pointing us to His Word. In this case, it was to Ephesians 2:19. He told us we should not worry about what their future earthly citizenship would be. The thing that mattered was that their citizenship was in heaven. With that word from the Lord, we made the decision to bring them back to Taiwan for their high school days. Today, more than forty years after that decision was made, our whole family has ended up in the United States. Donald and I soon realized we would have to retire to the States since all our children, grandchildren and great-grandchildren were there. Our decision to bring our boys back to Taiwan for high school has never been regretted, and only eternity will reveal the blessings that resulted for so many through Triple C Camps.

CHAPTER 11

In His Presence is Fullness of Joy
"Come and hear, all you that fear God; I will declare what He has done for my soul." Psalm 66:16

"The Lord is good to them who wait for Him; to the soul who seeks Him." Lamentations 3:2

NOTE: This testimony was first published in the September 1960 issue of Bread of Life, put out by the Ridgewood Pentecostal Church of Brooklyn, New York. This chapter is a flashback to November 1959, when the Lord reached down to me in a new and wonderful way. All the verses used come from either the King James or New King James Version of the Bible.

Almost seven months have passed since that glorious Lord's Day morning when Jesus Christ Himself, the great Baptizer, came to me before daybreak and baptized me with His Holy Spirit. I can never thank Him enough, or ever cease to praise Him for meeting me in this way. I would like to share with you my testimony: the events that led up to my Lord manifesting Himself and the events that followed. To Him be all the honor and all the glory; praise His holy name!

Since childhood days, I have always had a great desire to know God. I have been drawn to those who knew Him and longed to know Him myself. At the age of twelve years, I accepted Jesus Christ as my Savior. It was always my desire to be a missionary. With this purpose in view, I trained as a nurse during World War II. All through those student years I longed to know the Lord Jesus Christ better--my heart was drawn out to Him. A few months after the war ended, I was married to my "doctor" husband, and we set our eyes toward Inland China and, later, Formosa.

The Lord is so faithful. All through these years He has continued to draw me with His cords of love. Sometimes I was more conscious of this, and sometimes less. There were times when I made clear and definite steps of surrender—further dedication to the Lord. After these times, there would be a time of more intimate fellowship with Him. But, this never lasted, and I was not fully satisfied. For years I saw in God's Word a different kind of Christian life from the one I was experiencing—a life of victory over sin, a life where I could say, "It is no longer I who live, but Christ who lives in me" (Gal. 2:20). During the summer of 1959, a series of circumstances led up to my becoming really desperate to know a victorious Christian life. I had problems, yes, but above all else I longed to be victorious over the "sins that do so easily beset us," and I longed to know Jesus Christ in a deeper, fuller way.

One night, the Lord very clearly began telling me to get away by myself, for He wanted to speak with me. Two days later, the Lord led me to write in my diary (I had kept it only spasmodically since the beginning of the year): "Is my lack of faithfulness, my lack of power and victory in everyday life, because I have never been baptized with the Holy Spirit?" This question was implanted in my heart by the Spirit Himself. Until a few days prior to this, when I heard a close friend's testimony on how she had been filled with the Spirit, the Person and work of the Holy Spirit had not been anything I had ever considered in a personal way. I wrote in my diary that night: "Once again I affirm that my deepest desire and longing is to be utterly taken up with Jesus Christ Himself. Laying aside everything, that I may know Him, asking the Lord to fulfill in me all that is meant by being baptized with the Spirit, and filled with the Spirit."

A week later the Lord took me away alone. That first night I again wrote, "My one desire is to hear the Spirit's voice. What does He want to say to me, to do for me, in me, and by me?" After telling the Lord I was willing to listen to anything He said, I went to bed.

That week I spent almost the whole time alone with the Lord. He led me through the Word. Some verses stood out especially clearly: "John indeed baptized with water, but you shall be baptized with the Holy Spirit" (Acts 1:5, 11:16); "Be filled with the Spirit" (Eph. 5:18). He taught me Himself, step by step, until I knew and there was no longer any question in my heart that I needed to be baptized with the Holy Spirit.

The fourth day, I took a definite step of faith, standing on the promise in Luke 11:13, "If you then, being evil, know how to give good gifts to your children: how much more shall your heavenly Father give the Holy Spirit to them that ask Him?" I asked, and I believed that He gave. But, I also saw from God's Word that there always seemed to be some clear evidence to those around when people had been filled with the Spirit, and I just trusted the Lord for this evidence in His own time.

Saturday was, in many ways, a day of battling with the enemy. Satan sought to break me down, but praise the Lord! He is Victor! Finally, I went to bed that night with great peace in my heart.

Very early on Sunday morning, the Lord stood by me. He told me that He had come to give me power to witness (c.f. Acts 1:8 – "You shall receive power, after that the Holy Spirit is come upon you"). Then He spoke to me concerning many future things, revealing to me things that would happen in coming months, much of which was fulfilled within the next eight weeks. He also gave me a message for one of the local churches that met a specific need, although the need was quite unknown to me at the time. Finally, I had a very wonderful vision of the Lord's last days on earth: the days leading up to the Cross, the Resurrection morning, and the Ascension. Then, as I saw Him seated in heaven, I heard a clear voice telling me that He had sent the Holy Spirit to those who asked.

What more wonderful confirmation could there be than the Lord's own Word? My heart was overflowing in praise, worship and love. He filled my whole being. I knew as I had never known before the overwhelming joy of close, intimate fellowship with Christ, my Lord. I sang for a long, long time. My heart overflowed in love, adoration and praise. The words of a hymn, in measure at least, describe that hour: "lost in wonder, love and praise."

This was the evidence for which I had asked the Lord. His precious gifts, manifested at that time and abundantly proved in later weeks and months, are His way of telling others that He has baptized me. Not many weeks later, the Lord again manifested Himself to me and taught me more about the gifts of His Spirit, but this is another story. That first Sunday morning, I did not understand all that my Lord was doing in me and through me. I did not understand the importance of the message He gave, nor the results that would follow. But, I knew He had done all that He had taken me away to do, and I was now ready to return home, "being confident, that He who had begun a good work in me would perfect it until the day of Jesus Christ" (Phil. 1:6). Praise His wonderful Name! Oh, the matchless grace of God given to His children! Oh, that we might love Him more and more!

Someone may ask, "What has been the result of all this? Has it made any difference to everyday life? Do you know victory now that you did not know before? Are you satisfied as you never were before?"

The answer to all these questions is "Yes." But that is not the greatest thing. Far above anything I had asked or thought has been the way in which the Holy Spirit has revealed Christ to me. Truly, the Holy Spirit does not speak of Himself, but bears witness of Jesus Christ. He has made the sweet presence of Jesus so real to me in these past months that it has been like living in heaven itself. I have become so conscious of the presence of Jesus moment by moment throughout each day. Truly, He is altogether lovely, the Chief among ten thousand, He is my Beloved, He is my Friend (Song of Solomon 5:10b, 16b). He is my life (Col. 3:4). Without Him I can do nothing (John 15:5). There have been times when I have been so conscious of the Lord's control that I just stood back and watched as the Lord has worked in a situation. I have seen how beautifully He works when I keep my hands off.

The peace and rest of living a life utterly yielded to His control has been marvelous. No longer planning this and that, yet knowing unmistakably His directing—knowing that until He reveals His will, I need not and dare not speak or move. A word spoken out of place can be disastrous and cause many to suffer. Every thought, word, and deed must be under His almighty control. I have learned that the Lord times our lives to the smallest details. To leave home a moment too soon can mean missing the one the Lord would have me see. To arrive too early at my friends' home can mean a lost opportunity for Him. His timing is perfect; praise His Name.

The difference in my prayer life has been very marked. Many times the Spirit has taken over and prayed through me far beyond anything I had thought. The Spirit Himself prays through us. When He takes over, we know that things have been accomplished in heaven and in individual lives. Several times the Lord has definitely led in praying for the sick, and definite healing has been given. The Lord has opened up new truths as a result of prayer and searching in His Word. Almost every truth revealed has been quickly followed by an experience in everyday life--putting the truth to the test, proving to me in experience, in my own life, that which He was teaching. It is so wonderful to sit at Jesus' feet and be taught by Him, and He delights to open His Word to all those who will take the time to be with Him! "Not as though I have already attained or am already perfect, but I press on, if so be that I may apprehend that for which also I was apprehended by Christ Jesus (Phil. 3:12)."

Further results of this close fellowship with the Lord Jesus have been a much greater fear of the Lord and much greater hatred of sin. There have been falls, there have been mistakes, but the Lord in His great mercy has made me so quickly conscious of sin, and given me such a hatred for it, that I could turn immediately to the Lord, confessing all and trusting Him for forgiveness. How wonderful to know "if we confess our sins, He is faithful and just to forgive us our sins and to cleanse us from all unrighteousness" (1John 1:9). We must not hesitate when the Holy Spirit reveals sin; we must confess it at once, cry to the Lord for forgiveness, and He will abundantly pardon. The mercies of the Lord are so great, we shall never comprehend them, but praise His name we can accept them with grateful hearts.

Since that day in November 1959, life is so different from what it was before; really, the two cannot be compared. It is the difference between holding the reins myself and Jesus Christ being in control, between a walk after the flesh and a walk in the Spirit, between defeat and victory. Victory is assured, for He is Victor. Hallelujah! "In His presence is fullness of joy, at His right hand there are pleasures for evermore" (Psalm 16:11). Oh, that many, many more of God's children may know this life of victory, fullness of joy, and fruitfulness that will result from it. This is the rightful heritage of every child of God. This is the revealed will of God. "Therefore, do not be unwise, but understand what the will of the Lord is--and be filled with the Spirit" (Eph. 5:17-18).

Many years after the above story, the Spirit fell one evening on the Junior High boys in one of the Triple C Camp dormitories. Apart from one of the youngest, who was already asleep, the others all came under deep conviction. The counselors in that particular dorm took the kids up to the chapel where some were crying and confessing sin in their lives, others were laughing with that wonderful Holy Spirit joy, and others were just overcome by the powerful presence of the Lord. The power of God was in our midst. I was called to the chapel and thrilled to see what God was doing. The following morning, before daybreak, I went back to the chapel just to be alone with the Lord. As I was kneeling in prayer, the Lord reminded me of my Easter vacation in 1937. I used to walk the lanes enjoying the beauty of the flowers, the colors of the butterflies, the glory of the clouds and the sky. The Lord's presence was all around me, and I would sing and sing in what I called my "baby language." I knew nothing of what the Bible calls "singing in the Spirit." I had never heard of speaking in tongues. Yet, I believe that the Lord showed me that day at that Triple C Camp, He had filled me with His Spirit way back then. I was thirteen years old, just like many of those young boys He was filling with His Spirit that night, in northern Taiwan so many years ago. Remember, the Word tells us, "those who hunger and thirst after righteousness shall be filled" (Matt. 5:6). Jesus is our Righteousness (I Cor. 1:30), He longs to fill us with His Spirit, to fill us with all the fullness of God. This is His command:

" . . . BE FILLED WITH THE SPIRIT."

Ephesians 5:18

CHAPTER 12

CHRISTIAN CLINIC
1951 to 1978

"My thoughts are not your thoughts . . . says the Lord."
Isaiah 55:8

In 1964, our home, which had been on the edge of town when we bought it, was now in a good residential area. We were only five minutes from the largest hospital in the city, less than ten minutes from Taipei International Airport, and only three houses away from one of the main north-south highways through town. The city had doubled in size. It had become of international importance, had a foreign community of thousands instead of tens, and Donald was the only foreign doctor in practice in Taipei at the time. The Lord's thoughts truly are not our thoughts, and His ways are higher than our ways. From every aspect this had become an ideal location.

All through the years we had had a clinic running side by side with his private practice, seeking to help the poor, as well as those who could pay (some more – some less) for the medical care given. The private practice virtually paid for the clinic practice, which was free. This had resulted in our becoming totally swamped. Every member of a family would want to see the doctor, when only one was actually sick. On the advice of Chinese friends, we began to charge a small registration fee, the equivalent of US 25 cents per person, for which a patient could see the doctor, get two weeks supply of medicine, any ordinary lab tests and so on. This was simply a way to control the numbers a bit, but, of course, it did also help to defray the costs. The clinic patients had to register by 1 p.m., and they had to tell the nurse whether they simply needed medication refills or if they actually wanted to see the doctor. Then, while the nurses prepared the medicines, Brother Chang from our local assembly preached the Gospel to them. Quite a number of these clinic patients came to know the Lord, and at a later date we were able to start a visitation program out into the villages. Since these patients were almost all Taiwanese, we asked Dr Heikki Tenhunen (who arrived from Finland to help us in January 1966) to study Taiwanese rather than Mandarin with a view of starting this follow-up program. We also taught one or two of our nurses to drive so they too could help and the program would not totally depend on a westerner being available.

"Can we be baptized?" became quite a frequent question. What a joy it was to say, "Yes," to those who truly had given their lives to the Lord. Sometimes we could introduce them to a church nearby their home, and the local pastor would shepherd them from then onwards. On one occasion, Donald and several others from the clinic went climbing up a mountain to one of the more remote villages. Donald had asked if there was a small lake or any suitable place for an outdoor baptism and he had been told, "Oh, yes that is no problem." When they arrived, the baptistery turned out to be a small muddy pool with several buffalo in it enjoying the cool water in the hot afternoon sun! Nothing daunted, we baptized them with great joy. Afterwards, the group went into a tiny home where the owners took down the ancestor idol shelf and other objects linked with idol worship. The idols were taken outside and burned. In later years, when we traveled extensively in other parts of the world, I used to hear Donald describing our patient clientele as anyone from "Ambassadors to Aborigines" and our baptisms from Christian Clinic as "Baptisms with Buffaloes"!

Christian Clinic was open for twenty-eight years. The first eleven months were in rented property not too far from Mackay Memorial Hospital. After that, we moved to the property on Hsin Sheng South Road. One day, we had a letter from Dr. John Hobson in Burma. We were all at Barts together during the war, and his father was the preacher at our wedding. John wrote saying that Dr. Steven Chang and his family had to leave Burma because of the political situation. They had been working in the same mission hospital, and, since Dr. Chang spoke Mandarin, he planned to move his family to Taiwan.

"Could you help Steven find a job?" John wrote to Donald.

Once again we saw the provision of the Lord. We had been praying for another doctor to help Donald. Soon after Dr. Chang arrived in Taipei, he came to work part time at Christian

Clinic. Over the years our staff increased, and I have a 1968 report that states, "With the addition of an X-ray technician, the full complement of professional and technical staff totaled ten, two from abroad and eight local."

Soon after we moved to Hsin Sheng South Road, our first part-time voluntary evangelist came to preach to the clinic patients three afternoons a week. Later, in 1965, another part-time evangelist was added to the staff. As the Gospel outreach to these Taiwanese patients increased and Dr. Tenhunen's ability to speak Taiwanese also increased, we were able to have a regular visitation program. By 1971, we had over 11,800 registered clinic patients, all of whom would have heard the Gospel at least once. Most of them returned to the clinic many times with different members of their family.

From the beginning, our purpose at Christian Clinic was to help the Lord's children both medically and spiritually in any way we could. Our desire was to share with those who did not know Him the good news of Jesus Christ and His wonderful salvation. We did this in many ways. First of all, each member of our staff was a Christian and was encouraged to mature in the things of the Lord through our daily staff prayers. They were encouraged to share the light and love of the Lord with patients and fellow members of staff as He gave opportunity. Secondly, we had Christian literature in our waiting room, tracts that anyone who wished could take home with them, and Bibles available for anyone to read.

Another way we openly witnessed about being a Christian clinic was through the Scriptures we had written on both inside and outside walls. I remember when the Lord spoke to Donald and me very clearly one day from Deuteronomy 6:1-9. These verses tell of the tremendous importance of being careful to observe (hear and obey) God's Word. He is telling us to pass on His Word to our children and grandchildren. Then comes an interesting list of ways we are to do this. When we talk, when we walk, when we sit in our homes, when we lie down and when we rise up, we are to bind them on our hands and between our eyes. Then comes the final command, which is what caught our attention that day.

"You shall write them on the door posts of your house and on your gates."

We had, very recently, had a Chinese brother say to us, "If you ever want any signs written let me know, and I would be glad to do it for you." At the time we did not anticipate needing to take up his offer, but as we read those verses together we suddenly remembered what he had said. The result was that before long we had "I am the Way, the Truth, and the Life" written in Chinese on the beams of the shelter covering the area where the clinic patients sat and waited. At the other side of the house, which we called the front entrance, where our private patients came into the waiting room, we had written over the main door in bold letters the words "Jesus Christ is Lord."

It was not long after these Bible verses were written on "the door posts of our house" that I was attending a rather formal occasion in the foreign community, and a lady I did not recognize came up to me and introduced herself. She turned out to be the wife of a newly arrived ambassador in Taipei. She said, "You have no idea what an encouragement it was to me to walk into Christian Clinic and see written over the main entrance, 'Jesus Christ is Lord.' I just had to tell you." It turned out that she was a Christian and had been afraid, when she heard her husband was being sent to Taiwan, that she might be bereft of all Christian fellowship. The Lord allowed some minor medical problem to cause her to go and see the doctor and, through this, to find the Christians she had been praying she would find. She was greatly encouraged that day, and, of course, so was I.

Stories surrounding Christian Clinic and all that went on there are never-ending! Children loved Donald. The big jar of candies he had sitting on the windowsill helped. Any child who did not cry when Donald gave them a shot was given a candy. I am sure some that did not have a shot also got a candy from "Uncle Donald."

There were sad times at the clinic too. I vividly remember one Friday evening in the early seventies. We had just finished our weekly Friday night prayer meeting; most folks were still there in our home, when there was frantic ringing of our front doorbell. One of us opened the door and a distraught couple came rushing in with their little toddler in their arms. She had fallen into a small pool of water and drowned before anyone realized where she was. It was too late to resuscitate her.

But the happy times outweighed the sad times. Some of my happiest memories are of the Friday evening prayer meetings that became very much a part of the Christian Clinic's non-medical outreach. We were challenged by I Corinthians 14:26, "When you come together, everyone has a hymn, or a word of instruction, a revelation, a tongue or an interpretation. All of these must be done for the strengthening of the church." Why didn't our meetings look like that? On the first Friday evening of 1970, a group of about a dozen got together in our home, and we simply met around that word and asked the Lord to teach us. We had many surprises and learned many important truths from God's Word as we met together. Out of these meetings grew an early morning men's prayer group and, later, the three-day prayer retreats that were a blessing to many missionaries during the seventies. We learned together the joy of meetings when we put I Corinthians 14:26 into practice and really allowed the Spirit to lead us. These retreats were for men and women; they were held quarterly, alternating between long weekends and three days midweek. This accommodated those working in churches that preferred midweek and those teaching in schools.

After these Friday evening meetings had been going for just over a year, a Lutheran evangelist from Minneapolis came to Taiwan. Donald, along with some 30 to 40 other missionaries, gathered in one of the Lutheran student hostels. The speaker,

Brother Mjorud, shared his own testimony of salvation and of being baptized in the Holy Spirit. Donald's comment afterwards was that he had never before heard such clear, Biblical teaching on the baptism of the Holy Spirit. After the message, Brother Mjorud asked if there were anyone who needed prayer, for any reason. A dear Catholic sister said she had come believing that the Lord would fill her with His Spirit that very evening, and as they prayed, she began to sing praises to the Lord in a beautiful "new tongue." Then others asked for prayer. Quite a number were filled with the Spirit; some spoke in tongues for the first time. Donald asked for healing "for his voice" (which had suddenly left him a few hours earlier) and also for his asthma. His voice did not return for another four days, but his asthma was instantly healed. Donald used to say it seemed that at the moment they prayed for him, the gift of faith was dropped from heaven into his heart and he KNEW he was healed.

Several weeks after that meeting, Donald was the main speaker at a weekend conference in central Taiwan. It was for Campus Fellowship leaders from universities all over the island. About an hour before the first meeting, the leader of the conference came to Donald and said, "It seems your interpreter is not going to be here this evening, and you will need to speak in Chinese." Donald never preached in Chinese; he said that he felt too limited, especially when he was teaching a group of university students and graduates. Once alone, he cried out to the Lord, "Lord, if ever I need to speak in tongues it is now! Please, please give me this gift this evening." That night he spoke freely in Chinese for a good hour. At the next meeting, the interpreter was there and Donald spoke in English. After the meeting, a number of students gathered round him and said, "Why didn't you speak in Chinese? Last night was so much better."

Donald often used this incident as an illustration of how the Lord brought him to the place of total abandonment. He was ready for the Lord to do anything in his life, even to give him the gift of tongues! He sensed that the Lord had given him a known language that night to meet a specific need. However, later he was also given an unknown language, which the Bible tells us is for edifying ourselves, but it is also for building up the church when the message is interpreted (I Corinthians 14:4-5).

From the time the Friday evening meetings started, we often read I Corinthians chapters 12, 13, and 14 together. We became more aware of the wonderful gifts the Lord has for us. After Brother Mjorud's visit, Donald's freedom from asthma was a great cause for rejoicing, and it also made us search the Scriptures again on the subject of healing. That summer of 1971 saw us travelling around the world. We had the joy and privilege of attending two family weddings: Andrew and Janet's in Plymouth, Michigan and Tony and Felicity's in south London, England.

Throughout the three months that we were travelling, Donald needed no medication and was totally free of all signs of asthma. Then a strange thing happened. We arrived back in Taipei, and

Donald picked up a bad cold from one of the other doctors. His asthma returned, and, from then on, he was never free of it again. In later years, we discussed it sometimes and both felt that, had we known then what we learned later of spiritual warfare, the situation might have been very different. We should have recognized the enemy's tactics, refused his onslaught, and gathered those of like faith around us to battle through to victory. Instead, Donald went back on his previous medications, and, in a sense, just accepted the status quo. I heard him in later years giving others very different advice from what he himself had done at that time. Hopefully, others were spared going through similar trials, because he was able to share the lessons he learned from this experience. "We wrestle not against flesh and blood but against the powers of darkness, against spiritual hosts of wickedness in heavenly places" (Ephesians 6:12).

I will end this brief summary of Christian Clinic by sharing how just as clearly as the Lord opened the doors to Taiwan in 1949 and for us to open the clinic in 1951, so, twenty-eight years later, He showed us that He wanted the clinic closed. The message that we were not to lean on our own understanding but to allow Him to direct our path (Proverbs 3:5-6) once again was indelibly imprinted on our minds. We were travelling in North America towards the end of 1976, and both Donald and I had an increasing sense that the Lord was telling us He wanted the clinic closed. I remember how surprised, perplexed, even concerned we were. Could we possibly be hearing the Lord right?

When we got back to Taiwan and told the clinic staff, who quickly told the patients, we nearly had a mutiny! It seemed we were choosing to close at a time when there had never been more blessing. To cut a long story short, nearly eighteen months passed before we finally closed our doors. God had spoken, and the blessing only came when we obeyed.

During that year and a half, we tried to buy other property; we tried to reason why we simply could not close our doors, and we ended up losing quite a large sum of money. Finally we said, "Lord, we will obey You at any cost." As soon as we acted on this, everything fell into place, and we rejoiced in the Lord's confirmation. It truly was His plan that we closed. At that moment we had no idea what the Lord had for us, but we knew to TRUST HIM and not to lean to our own understanding.

After a short leave, some further language study, and many opportunities for preaching and teaching the Word in Taiwan, the Lord clearly led us to move to Hong Kong. It later became clear that this step to work with the Vietnamese "Boat People" in the refugee camps was a necessary, preliminary step towards our return to China. Jian Hua Foundation was started by a group of Chinese Christian businessmen with a burden to help China. They needed a leader who spoke English and Chinese to implement their vision. Donald was already in Hong Kong and available for what was later going to be described as the culmination of his life's work.

In closing this chapter, I will share a few extracts from the many emails that came after Donald's sudden "promotion to Glory":

Dr. Dale delivered my son Tim. I was way overdue, and he and Penny came to MY HOUSE!!! No doctor does that anymore. We had no phone, and he was concerned. In the end, the delivery was an emergency. While being wheeled into surgery, I was trying to sing an old Keswick chorus, "Praise the Savior all who know Him" – I was stuck and couldn't think of the rest of the words. Suddenly, I felt myself being wheeled very swiftly, and a strong voice picked up the song and finished it. It was the doctor, who had just arrived. What a wonderful way to go into an emergency – with a singing, godly doctor! You don't see that very often these days either . . . I thank God on every memory of Dr. Donald Dale – for his dedicated life, friendly spirit, and what he has meant to the Brantingham family in sickness and in health.

This next email is from a couple that was in the American military in Taiwan. They were young Christians and became quite involved with us in Triple C and Bible studies with the teenagers. Years later, when travelling in the States, our paths crossed once again. Here is what they wrote:

We praise God that He allowed our paths to cross briefly a few months ago (1997), while you were visiting with Norm and Muriel

Cook. That memory is not only sweet, it remains a blessing to us because it was then that Donald told Richard about some new medication for his asthma that literally has changed Richard's life, and he is virtually symptom-free. We believe that was the hand of God through Donald for us.

Here's one more quote, from a Scottish missionary family we knew well in Taiwan. It is written by Blanche, for, as she puts it, "them both":

"There are precious memories of Donald, not the least being that he saved Boyd's life during his initial visit to Taiwan in 1970."

(Donald would be the first to say he was only the instrument used; it was the Lord who saved Boyd's life.)

CHAPTER 13

STEPPING INTO THE UNKNOWN
1978 to 1981

"'I know the plans that I have for you,' declares the Lord."
Jeremiah 29:11

What a blessing that the Lord knows what He has planned for us. That verse goes on to say He has plans to prosper and not to harm, plans to give us hope and a future.

We had been in the same place for twenty-eight years, with the same work. It was not easy to close it all down with no idea at all what the Lord had for us next. Although in one way this was hard, in another it was exciting to follow the Lord into the unknown. We rejoiced to have another opportunity to trust Him completely and let Him direct our path.

The Lord did a very special thing for Donald at this time. Father MacNutt had planned a three-day, English-speaking, teaching seminar in Hsin Chu starting the evening of May 31st, 1978. That was the very day the clinic was to close. Both Donald and I were registered to attend the seminar and needed to be down in Hsin Chu by mid-afternoon that day. This meant that we left the clinic immediately after lunch and left Dr. Cameron Tallach and the other members of staff to close the doors to the patients for the last time. Donald and I were busy with the

MacNutt team, and, after the seminar, were to continue on with him to other parts of the Island to help the other team members who did not speak Chinese. This took away a lot of the sting and sadness of shutting down what had been our main work for so many years. The Lord is very gentle with His children, and I know that, for Donald especially, this was a big blessing. Looking back now, I see that the Lord had great plans for our future and the future of the many Vietnamese "Boat People" who would come to know Him in the Hong Kong refugee camps. At that time, we could not see this, but He had said His plans were to prosper us, and to give us hope and a future. His Word was wonderfully fulfilled beyond our wildest dreams in the following years. What surprises He had in store for us!

After the three days in Hsin Chu for MacNutt's English-speaking seminar, we went around the Island with his team for the Chinese meetings and enjoyed rich fellowship as we learned more lessons from God's Word on the matter of healing. Then we went back to Taipei for the rest of June to see Christian Clinic disbanded. Much of our equipment was given to Dr. Stephen Chang for his clinic, and the rest was dispersed to other clinics around the Island.

A wonderful four months followed in England. The whole family gathered, first of all at Tony and Felicity's home in London, and then at a lovely holiday hotel run by Christians in the southwest of England. All told, we were together as a family for almost three weeks. After that, Andrew and his family went home, and Robin went off on a business trip to the States. Then Donald and I visited many friends, went to several conferences meeting up with prayer partners, and got re-acquainted with those who had been so faithfully praying for us over many years, including those at Honor Oak. By the middle of November we were back in Taiwan and into regular language study each morning. Donald had many opportunities on Sundays to preach in different churches. Also, during this time he was teaching in student conferences and weekly Bible studies in the Taipei Medical College as well as several other centers.

In the spring of 1979, I was asked to take two babies to Holland for adoption. The two Dutch families involved covered all my expenses, as I travelled from Taipei to London, stopping in Amsterdam on the way. After a little time in London at Tony's home, I flew on to Detroit to see the rest of the family. No one was more surprised than I was when, on my first Saturday in Michigan, I received a phone call from Donald, who was in Hong Kong.

"I have been asked by Hong Kong Christian Service to become Medical Officer for the two refugee camps for which they are responsible to provide adequate medical coverage. Would you pray about staying in Hong Kong for the next year?" Then he suggested I should phone him back the next day with my comments, after I had time to think and pray about it. I phoned back the next day saying, "Yes," although there was a struggle in my heart over the decision.

My plane ticket, London to Detroit and back, for which we had initially put out the money, was all covered by belated tax refunds from my mother's estate, which arrived at Tony's address the very day I was again passing through London to return to the Far East. What perfect timing for that money to reach me, nearly five years after my mother died in Taiwan. I stopped off in Hong Kong for some days with Donald and then flew back to Taipei to pack up our home there. Fortunately, Robin was in Taipei and could help me, because Donald went straight to work in the refugee camps where the needs were unimaginably great.

For the next two years, he concentrated on the work in the camps. During this time, a number of refugees who were trained doctors, nurses, lab technicians and others, were allowed by the Hong Kong government to work with Donald and the others in the clinics, as long as there was a Hong Kong licensed doctor or nurse there on duty. Of those who worked with Donald, all but one became Christians before moving on to their host country. Even the one who did not believe when he left later gave his life to the Lord. Donald was quite free to have staff prayers every morning, just as we had had at Christian Clinic in Taipei. In fact, it was encouraged and enjoyed by all concerned.

After a while, a Sunday church service was also started and was attended by others in the camp, not just those who worked in the clinic. We had several baptisms in the sea during those two years, and we rejoiced that they were fruitful years for the Kingdom of God.

Early in 1981, while Donald was working with the Vietnamese refugees, three Chinese Christian businessmen approached him. They asked if he would consider giving up his medical work to come to work with them in a new charitable organization. They had just registered with the Hong Kong government under the name of the Jian Hua Foundation. (Jian Hua means to "build China.")

These men asked Donald to go into China with them in April 1981 to meet officials in Beijing and to discuss their plans. They made it known from the start that they, the three Board Members who had started Jian Hua, were all Christians and that anyone Jian Hua sent into China would also be a Christian. They would, however, be careful to obey the constitution of China that said no one was allowed to publicly propagate their faith, but it was understood if questions were asked, one could freely answer them. They expected to start helping in the medical field; this was partly why they had approached Donald. They also saw the need to help in all areas of the Four-Modernization Program that was much talked about in China in the early eighties. The Four-Modernization Program began with Deng Xiao Ping in 1978, and referred to modernizing four things: agriculture, industry, science & technology, and defense.

Teachers of English for the universities would be greatly appreciated for both long-term and short-term summer activities. Short-term medical seminars would also be acceptable. Donald returned from that trip feeling this request was certainly the Lord's next open door for us. Our first reaction was the joyful expectation that we would be able to go and live once more inside China. The Lord, however, challenged us at that point.

"Are you going to go, just the two of you, and live and work in one small area of China? Or, are you willing to look for and help others to go, so multiplying yourselves many times over?" This direct challenge from the Lord clearly set our course, and we said, "Yes," to the Lord. "Show us how, Lord. What would you have us to do?" On completion of his second year's contract with Hong Kong Christian Service, Donald began his work with Jian Hua in July 1981. By that time, many of the refugees had been offered homes in other countries, and also more doctors and nurses had been found to work in the camps. The need was no longer quite so critical, so Donald felt free to leave.

I have called this section of our story "Stepping into the Unknown," because when we closed Christian Clinic we had no idea what the future held. We only knew we had to obey the Lord, and He knew the plans He had for us. This knowledge gave us great peace. Now looking back, I see so clearly that if we had not closed the clinic we would not have been available to help the Vietnamese "Boat People." If we had not been with the Boat People there in Hong Kong at the time Jian Hua was beginning, Donald would not have been available when asked to be the first coordinator. The Lord who knows the end from the beginning had it all planned out.

Donald's mandate with Jian Hua Foundation was twofold: find Christian professionals from around the world with a heart to serve the Lord in China, and find places in China where they could serve. Our three friends who comprised the Jian Hua Board had been in touch with a few people they knew in the United Kingdom and the States. They gave a small file with a few letters to Donald who wrote to each person to find out their level and area of interest.

The thought then came to us, "We have hundreds of names and addresses on our personal letter list. Why not send all of them a letter telling of this new opportunity and the wonderful open door, and ask them to pass the word along." We did this, and we were thrilled with the quick and positive response that we had from so many.

So the ball started rolling, and it did not take long to see increased momentum. English teachers could usually be placed quite quickly. The other doors opened up more slowly, but over the next few years student summer camps became one of the most popular and effective ways of placing people in China. Teams of medical specialists were also able to give one and two week seminars at different medical colleges in a wide variety of cities.

How was all this fulfilling the goal to spread the gospel in China? Let me tell you a few real life stories:

After a long day of lectures and demonstrations in a medical college in the far northwest, our doctors were leaving the medical school building to walk across the campus to where they were staying. Once out in the dark, one of the Chinese doctors quickly caught up with Donald and the Australian doctor he was walking with.

"Please, can I ask you a question?"

"Of course," our doctors said, as they all walked on.

"I work in the oncology unit and see many of the patients dying. Why is it that the only ones who are not afraid to die all call themselves Christians?"

Questions like this one often resulted in one more soul entering the Kingdom, as was the case with this oncologist. In later years, when Donald was able to re-visit that medical college, that doctor was still growing in his faith, and he was incredibly happy to know the Lord.

On another occasion, Donald was staying in a hotel in one of the largest cities of China. A doctor came to visit him in his room. Just as the doctor stood up to leave, he pointed to the Bible on the bedside table. Donald always left his purposely, in an obvious place.

"Next time you come, please could you bring me one? I want my children to read it."

"Here, take this one," Donald said, handing it to him. "It is easy for me to get another one when I get home." Tears came to the doctor's eyes; of course, he wanted to read it too. He was thrilled to put it in his bag, well out of sight of anyone he might pass as he walked home.

As I write these stories, I have a large map of China on the wall beside me. It has hung on the wall in our various homes for almost twenty years. I am reminded of another incident when Donald was in the far southwest. The gentlemen who had been taking him round to visit the various authorities he needed to meet, was accompanying him to the airport on the last morning. They had been together several days, and now it was time for Donald to return to Hong Kong. After they got out of the limousine and out of earshot of the driver, our friend said to Donald, "Next time you come back, please bring me a Bible."

There is such a hunger in many hearts in China to read the Word of God. The sad part to this story is that Donald never had opportunity to return to that city. Whenever we thought of this incident, we prayed that the Lord would send someone else to provide a Bible for that man. I Corinthians 9:22-23 says, "I have become all things to all men so by all possible means I might save some. I do all this for the sake of the gospel, that I may share in its blessings."

These stories come from the early days of Jian Hua. Today we are not only placing English teachers and medical personnel, but agriculturists, specialists in computers, hotel chefs and those helping in major relief projects. Yes, Jian Hua is seeking to be all things to all men that, by all means, some may be saved.

I want to quote from a letter received this summer (2000) from a retired Taiwan missionary now in the States. He is commenting on my efforts to write this book as he says, "From the readers' point of view, the creation of Jian Hua and Donald's part in that, both from vision and medical involvement aspects, are intensely interesting, also up-to-date with present-day 'tent-making.' Of course, his early acquaintance with China, as well as life-long connection, prepared him for what crowned his earthly career."

I had never thought of Donald's part in Jian Hua in quite this way, but I believe that this is a beautiful tribute to the one who "took the (Jian Hua) ball and ran with it".

CHAPTER 14

WOMEN'S AGLOW FELLOWSHIP
August 1979 to February 1991

"Be aglow and burning with the Spirit, serving the Lord."
Romans 12:11b (Amplified)

"What is Aglow?" I have been asked many times. Our literature describes us as "a network of caring women." Our mission is "to lead women to Jesus Christ and provide opportunity for them to grow in their faith and minister to others."

August of 1979 found Donald and me in Hong Kong, as he began work with Hong Kong Christian Service in the Vietnamese transit centers, the camps set up by the Hong Kong government for the Boat People from Vietnam. We were living at my brother's home. The first morning, after Donald left for the camp and Neil for the school where he was working, I said to the Lord, "What am I supposed to do in Hong Kong?" I had always been active in Taiwan and did not want just to sit around. I was sure the Lord must have a job for me, too.

"Find the letter Jane Morrison sent you with all those names and telephone numbers," was the Lord's answer to me. I found it and saw about a dozen names and numbers. I started at the top of the list and phoned each lady. All who were home told me the same thing:

"On Wednesday we start three and a half days of training for future Aglow leadership. Come and join us."

"There are four leaders from Seattle coming to give the training. We want to become an affiliated Aglow chapter."

"We need all the help we can get at this time, if we are going to qualify."

One lady told me that registration to attend had officially closed, but she suggested that I phone the President, Kathy Landdeck, and see if I could still be included. She gave me Kathy's number. Each lady I spoke to that morning sounded so friendly and welcoming, and because they all told me about Aglow, I felt the Lord must want me involved. I called Kathy, and soon it was settled that I could join them for the training that started in two days time.

Those three and a half days sold me on Aglow! Our last morning, when we arrived at St. John's Cathedral, where the meetings were being held, we were all asked to sign up for the area in which we felt the Lord wanted us to help. I signed up for the Bible studies, saying I thought my brother would be happy for me to host a Bible study in his home, but I would have to check with him. Within a week or two, I had been asked to teach one of these studies, and then I was asked to be the Bible study coordinator, which automatically put me on the Hong Kong Aglow Board.

At our first monthly meeting, I put sign-up sheets on each table asking the ladies to sign if they would be interested in attending, hosting, or leading a Bible study. Many signed up, mostly for attending a study. I bought a map of Hong Kong, took three different colored crayons and, from the addresses on the sign-up sheets, marked where each lady lived. It was interesting to see the little clusters of ladies in different areas of Hong Kong and Kowloon, and there were hostesses in each area. It became apparent right away that we would need to find, or train, more leaders. I began by encouraging the areas where they did have a hostess and a leader to start right away. I visited each group, spotted potential leaders, and asked them to visit new groups that I taught myself for several weeks, and then had them lead. I would stay with them for a week or two until they became more confident. We trained up new leaders, and, at one point, we had more than a dozen Bible study groups actively meeting week by week. These Bible studies became the training ground for leaders in many areas of Aglow, in Hong Kong and other parts of the Far East, for a number of years.

The Hong Kong Bible studies were all in English for the first few years. There began to be more and more requests for Chinese studies as well, so, by the spring of 1984, a Cantonese monthly meeting had started and Jackie was their leader. As the Bible study coordinator, I met with her from time to time to give any help I could. One afternoon, when she came to our 28th floor little apartment, we had been discussing a number of issues when, suddenly, she said, "What we really need is a Bible study on the gifts of the Holy Spirit."

I agreed with her wholeheartedly, and we committed to make it a matter of prayer. Our question was this: Should the Aglow Bible study on the gifts of the Spirit be the first one to be translated? We thought it might well be the right place to begin.

Two days later, Donald returned home from the Jian Hua office with a large brown envelope in his hands. He passed it to me with a smile and the comment, "This is the Chinese translation of the Aglow Bible study, 'The Gifts of the Spirit.'"

"Where did you get that from?" was my amazed response. "Talk about 'before you call, I will answer you' (Isaiah 65:24). Is it possible that it's the whole book?"

It indeed turned out to be the whole book, and the story behind it is well worth sharing.

Some years before, Jean Swanson, of the Lutheran Mission in Taiwan, had visited Dr. Paul Yonggi Cho's church in Seoul Korea for a large conference. At one of the bookstores she had seen the Aglow Bible study on the gifts of the Holy Spirit. Since this was what she planned to teach at a Presbyterian ladies Bible study group when she returned to Taiwan, she decided to buy it. Impressed by the study, she and her co-worker translated it week by week to give to the ladies. Jean's co-worker was sister to Donald's office manager's wife, and the study had been sent from the sister in Taiwan to the sister in Hong Kong. Since the sister in Hong Kong knew I was working with Aglow, she had decided to give Donald a copy for me. She had no idea of our need, or the conversation between Jackie and me a couple of days earlier. Only the Lord could orchestrate such wonderful provision in such perfect timing. This meant we needed to consider checking the translation and then printing it as soon as possible. I contacted Aglow headquarters in Seattle. I received the all clear to go to Taiwan to look into this, with the help of Aaron Wong from the Elim Christian Bookstore. It was not long before we had our first Aglow Bible Study printed in Chinese traditional script and ready for use both in Hong Kong and Taiwan.

Over the next few years, a number of the small Aglow booklets such as "Tips for Speakers" and "Tips for Advisors" were translated and printed along with two more Bible Studies, "God's Daughters" and "Teach us to Pray." One year, Joan Morton, the leader of Aglow in Australia, brought a group of ladies to visit Hong Kong. They were to carry literature into China. The Australian Aglow covered the costs of reprinting in simplified script an excellent tract called "Receive All God Has to Give." This was something we had wanted to do anyway, and it was just one more example of the Lord's wonderful provision and timing.

As we got more material in Chinese, I was also able to take this into China where a number of individual Christians began to use the studies. Later, a Bible school requested quite a large number of copies of the study on the gifts of the Spirit, and for one whole semester they used this very successfully for teaching a class on the subject.

Some years later, an English-speaking group was started in Beijing, but, sadly, they had to be closed down after the tragic happenings in Tian An Men Square on June 4, 1989. Their executive committee of five represented four different countries, and at least three of them were told by their embassies that all women and children had to leave. The Seed of the Word had been sown, lives had been changed, and we know the Holy Spirit will continue His work in the hearts of those touched through Aglow and the Aglow literature at that time.

In November 1989, the executive board at headquarters in Seattle established what they called "Operation Link-up." The purpose is to encourage the more affluent fellowships in the west and down under to help the fellowships in the third world. They could help by prayer and by financial support. For example, the Australians had already provided much needed literature and visited and encouraged their sisters in both Hong Kong and China. Operation Link-up also resulted in the western fellowships becoming much more aware of the fellowships in the rest of the world. At the international and Asian conferences, sisters from different countries could meet each other, learn more of each other's needs, understand the specific difficulties in the different countries and commit with greater understanding to pray for one another. For example, most westerners do not understand the intricacies of Chinese writing. We can translate, then print, and whether the person reading the translation speaks Mandarin, Taiwanese, Cantonese or any other less-used dialect, the meaning of the characters they read is identical and written exactly the same way. So, even if the Chinese cannot understand each other's spoken language, they can write to each other and be perfectly understood.

A complication has arisen in recent years, because the Chinese mainland government tried to simplify the script. Today, however, most educated Chinese can read the traditional and simplified script, so it is becoming less of a problem. Many friendships have been made through meeting at the different conferences and then keeping in touch.

For me, Aglow became another wonderful vehicle for teaching the Bible and helping others experience just how practical God's Word is. Romans 12:11 (Amplified version), "Never flag in zeal . . . BE AGLOW AND BURNING WITH THE SPIRIT, serving the Lord," took on new meaning. I began to teach the Aglow women these Biblical truths to help them in both spiritual and practical areas of life. His Word is indeed both spirit and life (John 6:63).

CHAPTER 15

JIAN HUA EXPANDS ITS MINISTRY
1981 to retirement and beyond.

"I have been constantly on the move."
II Corinthians 11:26a (NIV)

The interesting little phrase I quote above is taken from the Apostle Paul's writings and accurately describes our eleven years with Jian Hua. In the King James Version it says, "In journeys often." Either version describes our days with JHF when we constantly traveled. Donald was travelling on his own to begin with. He was introducing the foundation to the States; most people had never heard of Jian Hua, and they found the name hard to remember. But, since this was a Chinese group registered in Hong Kong with Chinese leadership, we kept using the Chinese name. Today I believe that this was an important precedent. It has helped us in China and is beginning to help now as we are seeking to send more Chinese who live in western countries to be tentmakers in China.

After about a year, when our registration had come through, we actually had westerners living and working in China, then Donald also travelled there. He was visiting to help and encourage those already placed and to explore universities to find out in what areas they would appreciate Jian Hua's help. We were mostly asked for English teachers during our first few years, but later many other doors opened for both long-term and short-term personnel. Summer camps also became popular with native English-speaking students from around the western world. They were paired off with Chinese students who were majoring in English and delighted in having a month-long opportunity to live, work and play with those who only spoke English. These camps were held on the campus of the university from which the Chinese students came, and reports came back to us from their teachers of the tremendous improvement just one month being immersed in English had made.

To summarize these years of travelling, both in many parts of China and in an amazing number of countries around the world, is difficult. In China, we literally have been to the north, south, east and west. Perhaps more to the far northwest, Xinjiang, than anywhere else, but also often to Beijing and Tianjin. Through these years we have seen doors opening in so many different universities, as well as other schools and sometimes businesses. In the south, we were given a warm invitation to send doctors and nurses to the Wu Jing Fu hospital where Donald's father had worked years ago. Donald said we would love to help them, but they must first get a provincial guarantee that our western medical staff would be given a license to work there. Sadly, to this day, that has not come through.

I will now give you a summary from the last letter Donald wrote for Jian Hua before his official retirement in September

1992:

We have seen this work grow from its very humble beginnings in 1981, with only one full-time staff member [Donald] and a board of only three directors, until today [September 1992] when we now have: nine Directors on the Hong Kong Board, eighty adults serving inside China, four other national Boards of Directors, five voluntary secretaries serving in Australia, Canada, the UK and the USA (2), and six full-time staff in our H.K. office.

As I write this in December 2000, eight years after Donald retired, there is much further expansion under the excellent leadership of Peter Anderson who joined Jian Hua staff in 1991. The sad part is that there are far more open doors, especially for English teachers, than there are people volunteering to go to China. This is a matter for urgent prayer.

For Donald and me, the travelling did not come to an end with our so-called "official retirement" to Austin, Texas. In fact, if anything, it increased, and we could continue to say, "I have been constantly on the move." In 1993, we were away from Austin for seven months. We took a delightful trip to Taiwan, seeing many friends and experiencing the joy of a Christian Clinic staff reunion in Taipei. It was a wonderful holiday. Then we went to the all-Island Taiwan Missionary Conference in Taichung, and Donald was recognized as officially "retiring" even though it was fourteen years since we had left Taiwan. This all brings back happy memories. We went on to Hong Kong for some weeks staying in a "leave flat," loaned to us by friends who were away on leave. They also left us a car to use, which was such a blessing. From Hong Kong, we flew on to England. I remember remarking to Donald as we were flying, "When we left UK in 1948, it took us twelve weeks to the day before we arrived in China. Now we are taking twelve hours from Hong Kong back to England." That was a direct flight; we did not touch down anywhere. What a difference after forty-five years!

Over the next three months, we were travelling in many parts of England and Scotland, speaking on behalf of Jian Hua. This set the pattern for the following five years. In 1993, '95 and '97, we returned to the Far East for approximately three months each summer. In the intervening years we traveled in the States, Canada and UK also seeking to promote the work in China and the tremendous opportunities for the Lord that would arise if Christians would only get the vision of what true tentmakers can do in today's world.

Perhaps this sounds like "all work and no play," even in our retirement. It was not. During our last long trip in the U.S. in the fall of 1997, we had the tremendous joy of seeing and often staying with retired missionaries from Taiwan and ex-Triple C kids. Most of the latter were married, with children, and serving the Lord in many different capacities. We had much enjoyment and encouragement all along the way. During this trip, my right hip replacement, from January 1986, was giving me more and more trouble, and I was walking about with a cane most of the time. A phone call to Tony in Austin to ask him to contact the orthopedic surgeon I had previously seen, ensured that when we returned he would be able to operate without too much delay. By the end of November, I had my right hip-replacement surgery for the second time. This has been wonderfully successful, and today I walk again with no stick, no wheelchairs at the airports, and praising the Lord for His marvelous intervention.

When not "constantly on the move," we really enjoyed our "Retirement Cottage" as we called our home in south Austin. We got to know many of our neighbors, started a monthly neighborhood prayer meeting and were involved with Family Worship Center helping in any way we could. The prayer meeting started after we had walked up and down the immediate streets in our neighborhood for some weeks noticing different indications that certain families were Christians. Either a church name stuck on the back of a car, or a sign in a window would reveal brothers and sisters in Christ. One family with two cars outside particularly caught our attention.

"I love my wife," was on one and "I love my husband," was on the other!

We collected the names and addresses and sent everyone an invitation to our home for a certain evening. This was the beginning. I mention this to give you an idea you might want to try in your neighborhood, too.

Having Tony and his family only a seven or eight minute walk away was another great joy. We could pop in when passing by and keep in much closer touch than we had been able to before. We saw the other members of the family as we traveled in their areas. It was wonderful to see more of our sons, their wives and all our grandchildren after so many years of living far away. Our retirement years were happy years, and it was a delight to still be healthy and strong enough to be "constantly on the move" for the Lord. The last letter Donald wrote, in January 1998, mentioned that I was having some sporadic spikes of high blood pressure. He was feeling better than he had felt in a long time. He often said that retirement must be good for him. Little did he, or any of the rest of us, know, a few weeks later the Lord was going to take him to his "Heavenly Home."

On Tuesday, February 10th, Donald had some discomfort and what he described as "acid regurgitation" which he noticed most when lying down. He had been to see the family doctor and had quite a thorough examination. Nothing particular was found, and he was as active as usual. On Thursday, Tony and Felicity came to eat lunch with us, which was most unusual because they normally came Fridays at noon. As far as any of us can remember, that was the first time we had ever made that change. That afternoon, Donald and I were out grocery shopping together. When bedtime came, he said he would start the night in his chair in the living room where he could be more upright. At midnight, he came to bed saying he felt so much better that there was no point in being in the chair; he was much more comfortable in bed. We had a short conversation together and both went back to sleep. Around 4 a.m., I woke and, at first, thought he was snoring, which he often did, but then I realized it was not normal snoring sounds that I was hearing, and I sat up and put on the light. Quickly, I saw that he was deeply unconscious although still breathing. I could not find any pulse, and his breathing was becoming shallower. I phoned Tony and called EMS, but before either had arrived, and both came very quickly, Donald had stopped breathing. As he took his last breath, the Lord clearly said to me, "'Enoch walked with Me, and he was not, because I took him' (Genesis 5:24). Donald has walked with Me many years, and now he is no longer with you, I have taken him."

In that moment, such peace filled my heart that all I could do was thank the Lord that He had taken Donald with no pain, no suffering or sickness—what a wonderful, wonderful way to be taken into the presence of the Lord.

Of course it was a great shock to me, and to all our family and friends worldwide. There were the tears and moments of intense loneliness. But, through it all, God's word to me at that moment when He took Donald has been a constant comfort and joy. It is so beautiful to know the Lord took him in His perfect timing. Another word He gave me within a few moments of His taking Donald was from Deuteronomy 32:4: "He is the Rock, His works are perfect, and all His ways are just. A faithful God who does no wrong, upright and just is He." How precious are God's words to us in times like these.

Because God's Word has been so much a part of my life for so many years, I think it was only natural that when I found it hard to be alone at mealtimes I found my mother's copy of Daily Light. I kept it on the table where I ate, and I read and meditated on God's Word every time I sat down to eat alone. Often, too, if I had a guest we would read it together and share thoughts about what we had read. One day in December of that same year, I was having lunch alone and meditating in Chinese, which was quite unusual, on this little phrase, "Yu ni-di Shen tong hsing" ("To walk with God"). As I was thinking about this and the priceless privilege of being able to walk with God day by day, the Holy Spirit clearly said to me, "Get paper and a pencil." I obeyed and sat down again at the table. The Spirit began to dictate to me a poem, which later on, as I read it over again and again, I realized was a beautiful summary of our lives and what walking with God really means. It is hard to capture moments like these in mere human words, but I want to end this story by sharing this poem with you, and I encourage you to keep walking with God, until He takes you Home.

Penelope Dale

To Walk with God

To walk with God
O what a priceless privilege;
To walk with God
Is life itself to me.
To walk with God
And know His constant fellowship,
How can it be?
He longs to walk with me.

To walk with God
And know He's there beside me
To guide, direct,
And clearly show the way.
To walk with God
And listen carefully to Him
Each word so precious
Oh! Help me to obey.

(Compare with Micah 6:8)